First World War
and Army of Occupation
War Diary
France, Belgium and Germany

27 DIVISION
81 Infantry Brigade
Princess Louise's (Argyll & Sutherland Highlanders)
1st Battalion
19 December 1914 - 31 October 1915

WO95/2263/2

The Naval & Military Press Ltd
www.nmarchive.com
Published in association with The National Archives

Published by

The Naval & Military Press Ltd

Unit 10 Ridgewood Industrial Park,

Uckfield, East Sussex,

TN22 5QE England

Tel: +44 (0) 1825 749494

www.naval-military-press.com

www.nmarchive.com

This diary has been reprinted in facsimile from the original. Any imperfections are inevitably reproduced and the quality may fall short of modern type and cartographic standards.

Contents

Document type	Place/Title	Date From	Date To
Heading	WO95/2263-2		
Heading	1st Bn Argyll & Suth'd Hdrs Dec 1914-Oct 1916		
Heading	1st Battn. The Argyll & Sutherland Highlanders. December 1914		
War Diary	Winchester	19/12/1914	19/12/1914
War Diary	Havre	20/12/1914	21/12/1914
War Diary	Aire	22/12/1914	31/12/1914
Heading	1st Battn. The Argyll & Sutherland Highlanders. January 1915		
War Diary	Aire	01/01/1915	06/01/1915
War Diary	Fletre	07/01/1915	07/01/1915
War Diary	Dickebusch	08/01/1915	08/01/1915
War Diary	Dickebusch Groenen Farm	09/01/1915	10/01/1915
War Diary	Elzenvalle	11/01/1915	13/01/1915
War Diary	Zevecoten	14/01/1915	14/01/1915
War Diary	Zevecoten Dickebusch	15/01/1915	15/01/1915
War Diary	Voormezele	16/01/1915	18/01/1915
War Diary	Dickebusch	19/01/1915	20/01/1915
War Diary	Elzenvalle	21/01/1915	21/01/1915
War Diary	Trenches Dickebusch	22/01/1915	22/01/1915
War Diary	Dickebusch Zevecoten	23/01/1915	23/01/1915
War Diary	Zevecoten	24/01/1915	28/01/1915
War Diary	Zevecoten to Dickebusch	29/01/1917	29/01/1917
War Diary	Dickebusch to Elzenvalle	30/01/1917	30/01/1917
War Diary	Elzenvalle to Trenches	31/01/1917	31/01/1917
Miscellaneous	Appendices		
Diagram etc			
Diagram etc		11/01/1915	11/01/1915
Miscellaneous	Operation Orders by Lieut Col. H.L. Henderson, Comdg. S. Highlanders	10/01/1915	10/01/1915
Heading	1st Battn. The Argyll & Sutherland Highlanders. February 1915		
War Diary	Trenches	01/02/1915	01/02/1915
War Diary	Trenches & Dickebusch	02/02/1915	02/02/1915
War Diary	Dickebusch	03/02/1915	03/02/1915
War Diary	Dickebusch to Trenches	04/02/1915	04/02/1915
War Diary	Trenches	05/02/1915	06/02/1915
War Diary	Elzonvalle	07/02/1915	08/02/1915
War Diary	Trenches	09/02/1915	09/02/1915
War Diary	Trenches Dickebusch	10/02/1915	10/02/1915
War Diary	Dickebusch Zevecoten	11/02/1915	11/02/1915
War Diary	Zevecoten	12/02/1915	14/02/1915
War Diary	Dickebusch	15/02/1915	15/02/1915
War Diary	Trenches to Dickebusch	16/02/1915	16/02/1915
War Diary	Dickebusch	17/02/1915	17/02/1915
War Diary	Dickebusch to Trenches	18/02/1915	18/02/1915
War Diary	Trenches	19/02/1915	19/02/1915
War Diary	Trenches to Dickebusch	20/02/1915	20/02/1915
War Diary	Dickebusch	21/02/1915	22/02/1915
War Diary	Dickebusch & Trenches	22/02/1915	22/02/1915

War Diary	Trenches	23/02/1915	23/02/1915
War Diary	Trenches to Dickebusch	24/02/1915	24/02/1915
War Diary	Dickebusch	25/02/1915	25/02/1915
War Diary	Dickebusch to Trenches	26/02/1915	26/02/1915
War Diary	Trenches to Zevecoten	27/02/1915	27/02/1915
War Diary	Zevecoten	28/02/1915	28/02/1915
Miscellaneous	Reports on Reconnaissances		
Miscellaneous	27th Division	21/02/1915	21/02/1915
Miscellaneous	Headquarters, 5th Corps	21/02/1915	21/02/1915
War Diary	Headquarters, 27th Division.	20/02/1915	20/02/1915
Miscellaneous	All reference to left or right of saps etc. refer to our own left or right.		
Diagram etc			
Miscellaneous	Headquarters, 5th Corps.	18/03/1915	18/03/1915
Miscellaneous	Reconnaissance from Brick Kiln in front of Mound 14-3-1915	18/03/1915	18/03/1915
Heading	1st Battn. The Argyll & Sutherland Highlanders March 1915		
War Diary	Zevecoten	01/03/1915	04/03/1915
War Diary	Zevecoten to Dickebusch	05/03/1915	05/03/1915
War Diary	Dickebusch	06/03/1915	06/03/1915
War Diary	Dickebusch to Trenches	07/03/1915	07/03/1915
War Diary	Trenches	08/03/1915	08/03/1915
War Diary	Trenches & Dickebusch	09/03/1915	09/03/1915
War Diary	Dickebusch	10/03/1915	10/03/1915
War Diary	Dickebusch to Trenches	11/03/1915	11/03/1915
War Diary	Trenches	12/03/1915	12/03/1915
War Diary	Trenches to Dickebusch	13/03/1915	13/03/1915
War Diary	Dickebusch to Elzonvalle	14/03/1915	15/03/1915
War Diary	Trenches	16/03/1915	18/03/1915
War Diary	Trenches to Dickebusch	19/03/1915	19/03/1915
War Diary	Dickebusch	20/03/1915	23/03/1915
War Diary	Canada Huts	24/03/1915	31/03/1915
Heading	1st Battn. The Argyll & Sutherland Highlanders. April 1915		
War Diary	Dickebusch	01/04/1915	03/04/1915
War Diary	Dickebusch to Trenches	04/04/1915	04/04/1915
War Diary	Trenches	05/04/1915	07/04/1915
War Diary	Trenches to Ypres	08/04/1915	08/04/1915
War Diary	Ypres	09/04/1915	11/04/1915
War Diary	Ypres to Trenches	12/04/1915	12/04/1915
War Diary	Trenches	13/04/1915	15/04/1915
War Diary	Trenches to Sanctuary Wood	16/04/1915	16/04/1915
War Diary	Sanctuary Wood	17/04/1915	20/04/1915
War Diary	Trenches	21/04/1915	30/04/1915
Heading	1st Battn. The Argyll & Sutherland Highlanders. May 1915		
War Diary	Trenches	01/05/1915	18/05/1915
War Diary	Trenches to Bivouacs near Basse Boom	19/05/1915	19/05/1915
War Diary	Bivouacs	20/05/1915	23/05/1915
War Diary	Bivouacs to Support	24/05/1915	24/05/1915
War Diary	Huts H 11 C	25/05/1915	27/05/1915
War Diary	H 11 C to Locre	28/05/1915	28/05/1915
War Diary	Locre to Le Petit Mortier	29/05/1915	29/05/1915
War Diary	Le Petit Mortier to Trenches I 21 A	30/05/1915	30/05/1915
War Diary	Trenches	31/05/1915	31/05/1915

Heading	1st Battn. The Argyll & Sutherland Highlanders. June 1915		
War Diary	Trenches Rue De Bois 7 I. 21	01/06/1915	01/06/1915
War Diary	Trenches I. 10	02/06/1915	02/06/1915
War Diary	Trenches	03/06/1915	07/06/1915
War Diary	Trenches to Billets	08/06/1915	08/06/1915
War Diary	Armentieres	09/06/1915	09/06/1915
War Diary	Billets	10/06/1915	11/06/1915
War Diary	Billets to Trenches	12/06/1915	12/06/1915
War Diary	Trenches	13/06/1915	18/06/1915
War Diary	Billets	19/06/1915	23/06/1915
War Diary	Billets to Trenches	24/06/1915	24/06/1915
War Diary	Trenches	25/06/1915	29/06/1915
War Diary	Trenches to Billets	30/06/1915	30/06/1915
War Diary	During the Month of June and month in the 1/Aug 16 Mentioned in depatcher D.C.M Military Corps	30/06/1915	30/06/1915
War Diary	Red Ticket From g.o.c.27th green ticket from G.O.C. 27th	30/06/1915	30/06/1915
War Diary			
Heading	1st Battn. The Argyll & Sutherland Highlanders. July 1915		
War Diary	Billets	01/07/1915	05/07/1915
War Diary	Billets to Trenches	06/07/1915	06/07/1915
War Diary	Trenches	07/07/1915	11/07/1915
War Diary	Trenches & Billets	12/07/1915	12/07/1915
War Diary	Billets	13/07/1915	17/07/1915
War Diary	Billets to Trenches	18/07/1915	18/07/1915
War Diary	Trenches	19/07/1915	24/07/1915
War Diary	Trenches to Billets	25/07/1915	25/07/1915
War Diary	Billets	26/07/1915	31/07/1915
Heading	1st Battn. The Argyll & Sutherland Highlanders. August 1915		
War Diary	Armentiers	01/08/1915	01/08/1915
War Diary	Armentiers to Jesus Farm	02/08/1915	02/08/1915
War Diary	Jesus Farm	03/08/1915	15/08/1915
War Diary	Jesus Farm to Trenches	16/08/1915	16/08/1915
War Diary	Trenches	17/08/1915	29/08/1915
War Diary	Trenches to Billets	30/08/1915	30/08/1915
War Diary	Billets Rue Delett Ree	31/08/1915	31/08/1915
Heading	1st Battn. The Argyll & Sutherland Highlanders. September 1915		
War Diary	Rue Delett Ree H 23 A Sheet 36	01/09/1915	05/09/1915
War Diary	Billets to Trenches Bois Grenier	06/09/1915	06/09/1915
War Diary	Trenches	07/09/1915	12/09/1915
War Diary	Trenches Bois Grenier	13/09/1915	14/09/1915
War Diary	Trenches to Jesus Farm	15/09/1915	15/09/1915
War Diary	Jesus Farm	16/09/1915	16/09/1915
War Diary	Jesus Farm to Bleu	17/09/1915	17/09/1915
War Diary	Bleu	18/09/1915	18/09/1915
War Diary	Bleu to Hazebrouck	19/09/1915	19/09/1915
War Diary	Hazebrouck to Lamotte En Santerre Amiens Sheet 12	20/09/1915	20/09/1915
War Diary	Lamotte on Santerre	21/09/1915	23/09/1915
War Diary	Billets	24/09/1915	26/09/1915
War Diary	Billets Lamotte En Santerre	27/09/1915	27/09/1915
War Diary	Billets	28/09/1915	30/09/1915

Heading	1st Battn. The Argyll & Sutherland Highlanders. October 1915		
Miscellaneous	A.G's Office 3rd Echelon Base	10/11/1915	10/11/1915
War Diary	Billets Lamotte en Santerre Map Sheet 12 Amiens	01/10/1915	01/10/1915
War Diary	Billets	02/10/1915	03/10/1915
War Diary	Lamotte to Chuignolles	04/10/1915	04/10/1915
War Diary	Billets Chuignolles	05/10/1915	05/10/1915
War Diary	Billets	06/10/1915	07/10/1915
War Diary	Billets to Trenches	08/10/1915	08/10/1915
War Diary	Trenches	09/10/1915	11/10/1915
War Diary	Trenches to Chuignolles	12/10/1915	12/10/1915
War Diary	Billets	13/10/1915	15/10/1915
War Diary	Chuignolles to Trenches	16/10/1915	16/10/1915
War Diary	Trenches	17/10/1915	20/10/1915
War Diary	Billets	21/10/1915	22/10/1915
War Diary	Chuignolles to Mericourt	23/10/1915	23/10/1915
War Diary	Mericourt to Lamotte on Santerre	24/10/1915	24/10/1915
War Diary	Billets	25/10/1915	25/10/1915
War Diary	Lamotte on Santerre to Boves	26/10/1915	26/10/1915
War Diary	Boues to Bougainville	27/10/1915	27/10/1915
War Diary	Billets	23/10/1915	31/10/1915

WO 95/2263/2

27TH DIVISION
81ST INFY BDE

1ST BN ARGYLL & SUTH'D HDRS

DEC 1914 - OCT 1915

~~ON LOAN TO MR WRIGHT~~

~~6 - JAN 1953.~~

V1.

81st Infantry Brigade.

27th Division.

Battn. disembarked
Havre from England
20.12.14.

WAR
DIARY

1st BATTN. THE ARGYLL & SUTHERLAND HIGHLANDERS.

D E C E M B E R

1 9 1 4

Instructions regarding War Diaries and Intelligence Summaries are contained in F. S. Regs., Part II. and the Staff Manual respectively. Title pages will be prepared in manuscript.

WAR DIARY
or
~~INTELLIGENCE SUMMARY~~
(Erase heading not required.)

Army Form C. 2118.

Hour, Date, Place		Summary of Events and Information	Remarks and references to Appendices
19th Dec	WINCHESTER	Paraded 3.30 a.m. Marched to Southampton. Embarked on H.T. NOVIAN. Officers embarking. Lt Col Henderson commanding. Maj Gore. Capts Sceales, MacEwen, Porteous, Wilson. Lts Patten, Young, Purvis, Stirling. 2/Lts Steel, Ritchie, Clarke, Greenfield, Kincaid-Lennox, Murray, Graham, Gibb, Forbes Leith, Macdonald, Neill, McCutcheon, Rowan, Thomson, Bolton, Rome. Lt & QrMr Heatly. Rank & file. M.O. Lt Selby RAMC	ARB
20th Dec	HAVRE	Disembarked. Marched to St ADRESSE rest camp HAVRE	ARB
21st Dec	HAVRE	Entrained for front.	
22nd Dec	AIRE	Arrived at AIRE. Marched to billets. Men billetted in LA POUDRIÈRE. Officers in various houses. Billets on the whole comfortable	Ref Map ST OMER No 4. ARB
23rd Dec	AIRE	Settling down into billets. Quiet day.	ARB
24th Dec	AIRE	Xmas Eve. Brigade route march. Lt & Adjt A.R. Boyle rejoined from sick leave	ARB
25th Dec	AIRE	Xmas Day. Company training. All ranks delighted with Their Majesties and Princess Mary's presents and Daily News plum puddings	From King & Queen. Card from Princess Mary. Box containing pipe, tobacco, cigarettes & card. ARB
26th Dec	AIRE	Company training. Interior economy.	ARB
27th Dec	AIRE	A & B Coys commenced line of entrenchments East of BOESEGHEM where whole Brigade was situated. Worked on left of 2nd Camerons. Good work done notably by A Coy. C & D Coys relieved A & B at 1 p.m. Very cold wet day.	ARB

11

Instructions regarding War Diaries and Intelligence Summaries are contained in F. S. Regs., Part II. and the Staff Manual respectively. Title pages will be prepared in manuscript.

WAR DIARY
or
INTELLIGENCE SUMMARY
(Erase heading not required.)

Army Form C.

Hour, Date, Place		Summary of Events and Information	Remarks and references to A
28th Dec.	AIRE	Line of entrenchments continued to South. Ground wet and work difficult. Same routine as on previous day. Good revetting by C Coy.	ARB
29th Dec	AIRE	Trenches begun S of PECQUEUR in continuance of scheme. Ground very difficult. Owing to wet it was impossible to dig down; so companies built up. Progress slow. Vile weather continued	ARB
30th Dec.	AIRE	Entrenching scheme continued on section started on 27th Dec. Cover trenches, latrines etc made. Much drainage necessary. Captain Sceales Lt Purvis; C. S. Whitehill. Sgt Muller left for trenches for experience	ARB
31st Dec	AIRE	As on 29th Dec. Good revetting work by B Coy.	ARB

V 2

81st Infantry Brigade.

27th Division.

WAR DIARY

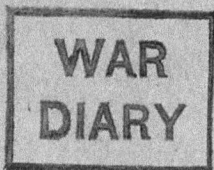

1st BATTN. THE ARGYLL & SUTHERLAND HIGHLANDERS.

J A N U A R Y

1 9 1 5

Attached:

Appendices.

1st Battalion The Argyll & Sutherland Highlanders.

January 1915

1915 1st Jany	AIRE	C & D Coys continued trench work on Southern section stopping work at 12.30 p.m. Dinners eaten on ground. A & B marched out to join C & D – whole Battalion marched to ground E of BOESEGHEM where whole Brigade was inspected by Field Marshal Sir John French C in C accompanied by Sir H. Smith Dorrien G.O.C. 2nd Army, General T.D.O. Snow commanding 27th Division etc etc. Long wait & short inspection. Captain Scales & trench party returned full of experience.

A.W.B.

II

Original

1st Arg. Hrs [?]

Army Form C. 2118.

WAR DIARY
or
~~INTELLIGENCE SUMMARY~~

(Erase heading not required.)

Instructions regarding War Diaries and Intelligence Summaries are contained in F. S. Regs., Part II. and the Staff Manual respectively. Title pages will be prepared in manuscript.

91st

Hour, Date, Place	Summary of Events and Information	Remarks and references to Appendices
Jany 2nd 1915 AIRE	Digging scheme continued – also the filthy weather.	
" 3rd "	Half days work – Two coys. C & D only working	
" 4th "	Orders received to hold ourselves in readiness for early move to trenches	
" 5th "	Getting ready.	
" 6th "	Orders received overnight. Paraded 8.50 a.m. Marched via HAZEBROUCK to FLETRE where we billeted inspected on the road by Sir H. Smith Dorrien commanding 2nd Army. Tiring day. Roads nearly all pavé. Billets bad.	vide Sheet HAZEBROUCK 5A
" 7th FLETRE	Paraded 7.50 a.m. Very hard day. Marched via BAILLEUL and LOCRE to DICKEBUSCH (vide orders). First day of war in BELGIAN territory. About 2.30 p.m. ordered to halt as road was being shelled. Very bad weather – roads worse. After dusk marched into DICKEBUSCH by detour. Thence 1 mile N. by YPRES road. Billeted on that road. Billets far too small very dirty and still inhabited by French troops. Many houses had been wrecked by shell fire. Transport late and altogether a very uncomfortable night.	
8th DICKEBUSCH	Billets vacated before dawn and battalion marched W. to ~~crossroads~~ position 500x west of cross roads in square H 29 B. Took up positions near French guns along bank of canal. These had to be vacated soon owing to shell fire. A Company however dug itself into bank of canal with great success and did not move. German artillery searching for French guns all day. Returned to billets (which had been shelled by day) after dusk.	vide squared sheet YPRES

1247 W 3299 200,000 (E) 8/14 J.B.C. & A. Forms/C. 2118/11.

original

Army Form C. 2118.

Instructions regarding War Diaries and Intelligence Summaries are contained in F. S. Regs., Part II. and the Staff Manual respectively. Title pages will be prepared in manuscript.

WAR DIARY
or
~~INTELLIGENCE SUMMARY~~

(Erase heading not required.)

9th

Hour, Date, Place	Summary of Events and Information	Remarks and references to Appendices
Jany 9th DICKEBUSCH GROENEN FARM	As for previous day. Bad weather continued. Work done – cutting brushwood for revetment etc. Lt. Greenfield thanked by Brigadier General for excellent reconnaissance carried out on previous day, to establish positions of French troops.	vide squared sheet YPRES
10th "	Spent day at GROENEN FARM. Paraded 7.30 p.m. and marched east to KRUISSTRAATHOEK in support of the three other regiments of the Brigade. Relieved 4th Bn Rifle Brigade who were in comfortable billets in road KRUISSTAATHOEK – ELZENVALLE. Bad weather continues and march very slow. Billets palaces after last ones. Quiet night but for snipers. Brigade took over trenches from 80th Brigade without much loss.	vide sketch map K1 and march orders.
11th ELZENVALLE	Much artillery firing. Shells going over all day. D company being nearest to danger zone. Allies' guns particularly busy. Confined to billets all day working at improvement of trench. [illegible] etc all night. Telephone wires cut all day & night. Sniping heavy and fairly close.	

Part III page 1 original

Instructions regarding War Diaries and Intelligence Summaries are contained in F. S. Regs., Part II. and the Staff Manual respectively. Title pages will be prepared in manuscript.

WAR DIARY
or
INTELLIGENCE SUMMARY
(Erase heading not required.)

Army Form C. 2118.

Hour, Date, Place		Summary of Events and Information	Remarks and references to Appendices
Jany 12th 1915	ELZENVALLE	Fairly quiet day. Shell fire as usual. Companies worked by night at improvement of bombproofs etc. All billets vacated by French troops are indescribably filthy	
Jany 13th	ELZENVALLE	Quiet day. Relieved by 4th K.R.R. at 6.30 pm. Marched back through DICKEBUSCH to ZEVECOTEN near which place whole Battalion was billetted	
Jany 14th	ZEVECOTEN	Billets comfortable and a welcome change after previous week. Day of rest. Men at last got a chance of a wash. Officers owing to our interpreters efforts were able to use a hot shower bath admirably run by the French troops in an old Brewery.	
Jany 15th	ZEVECOTEN } DICKIEBUSCH }	Marched to DICKEBUSCH in evening. Dirty billets again.	
Jany 16th	VOORMEZELE	Marched in evening to relief of P.P.C.L.I. and part of K.S.L.I. in trenches. Left section of our line. Weather bad, but relief on the whole well carried out. "A" Coy had a little difficulty owing to absence of guides, and a connecting file being shot. Reports from Coys. good. Sniping heavy. Little shell fire	
Jany 17th	VOORMEZELE	Usual daylight life underground. Headquarters in a cellar of a ruined house. All houses in the small village seemed to have suffered. Dispositions as follows - Hd. Qrs. 1 M.G. in reserve nearly 2 platoons surplus from the trenches, M.O.'s temporary hospital in VOORMEZELE. Support centre of 1 platoon and 1 platoon in reserve in KRUISTAATHOEK. "C" Coy on left of line joining French trenches. ¾ B Coy in centre near ST ELOI with one M.G. "A" Coy on right with Gloucesters beyond. ½ D Coy in support. Shelling & sniping bad. Trenches in very bad state. Head cover nearly all broken down. Reliefs for worst trenches (C Coys) and ration parties went out at night. 2 Lt. A.M.C.D. Ritchie wounded in left shoulder	

1247 W 3299 200,000 (E) 8/14 J.B.C. & A. Forms/C. 2118/11.

2. Part III page 2 original

Instructions regarding War Diaries and Intelligence Summaries are contained in F. S. Regs., Part II. and the Staff Manual respectively. Title pages will be prepared in manuscript.

WAR DIARY
or
INTELLIGENCE SUMMARY

(*Erase heading not required.*)

Army Form C. 2118.

Hour, Date, Place	Summary of Events and Information	Remarks and references to Appendices
Jany 18th VOORMEZEELE	Heavy shelling all day. Hd Qrs & hospital both getting their share. The men who had done 24 hours in trenches fairly comfortable and very cheery. Relieved by Royal Irish Regiment in evening. Much shelling and sniping during relief. Companies marched back to DICKEBUSCH independently. Notes on first days in trenches. French trenches bad and dirty. Necessity to keep men employed all night, improving and adding to trenches. If in trenches 48 hours, men should take rations for that time, owing to difficulty of taking heavy boxes to trenches. Necessity of having intelligent guides - at least 2 per coy. Periscopes of any sort useful. 2/Lt Forbes Leith specially commended for good report on german position. Counter sniping and patrols to stop snipers. Vaseline for feet excellent. Stretcher bearers and M.O worked splendidly. Telephones a necessity. Casualties 3 men killed 1 officer 13 men wounded.	91st
Jany 19th DICKEBUSCH	Resting and cleaning up. Conference in Brigade office. Pte Bellingham A Coy died of wounds.	
Jan 20th DICKEBUSCH	Buried Bellingham. Some men employed digging another line of trenches. 'A' Coy to LA BRASSERIE at 4.30 a.m.	
Jan 21st ELZENVALLE	Marched to old billets here in relief of Leinsters. Relieved Camerons in trenches in the evening. Our first sight of the enemy! Two German sappers had lost their way, or deserted and had been taken by Camerons. A good deal of information was obtained from them. Relief was well carried out.	
Jany. 22nd Trenches DICKEBUSCH	A raid for snipers in the early morning was unsuccessful. No doubt that the only way to combat these pests is to snipe as well. Set a thief etc. Lovely day after frosty night. Aeroplanes very busy. Relieved by Leinsters about 8pm. Marched back to DICKEBUSCH. Casualties Killed Pte Blaikie A Coy died of wounds Pte Ferguson B Coy wounded	

Part III page 3. original

Instructions regarding War Diaries and Intelligence Summaries are contained in F. S. Regs., Part II. and the Staff Manual respectively. Title pages will be prepared in manuscript.

WAR DIARY
or
INTELLIGENCE SUMMARY

(Erase heading not required.)

Army Form C. 2118.

Hour, Date, Place		Summary of Events and Information	Remarks and references to Appendices
Jan 23rd	DICKEBUSCH } ZEVECOTEN }	Rested in morning. Marched via OUDERDUN to ZEVECOTEN for 6 days rest. In old billets. Very welcome rest.	
Jan 24th	ZEVECOTEN	Quiet day, cleaning up. Many men suffering from stomach trouble caused by cold and general filth. The Battalion less decimated than others in the Division. Office work very heavy for war-time	
Jan 25th	ZEVECOTEN	Companies under officers commanding. Men still cleaning up. Trench mud very difficult to get off. Luckily weather remains dry. Snipers busy even in this peaceful part. A great nuisance. Probably discontented Belgians.	
Jan 26th	ZEVECOTEN	A famous day. News in the papers of the sinking of the "Blucher" in North Sea - and - a hot shower bath [illegible] for all ranks in the French bathing room. Much appreciated and more than necessary. Several men report clothing verminous. N.B. Shirts very necessary rather than woollen comforters etc. Kaisers birthday tomorrow and an attack is expected. The enemy has been active against 1st corps at GIVENCY and French N. of YPRES. Both attacks repulsed. The latter notable as having had no preliminary artillery preparation - infantry advanced in dense masses very suddenly. C.O went to hospital in morning; several officers very seedy.	

Instructions regarding War Diaries and Intelligence Summaries are contained in F. S. Regs., Part II. and the Staff Manual respectively. Title pages will be prepared in manuscript.

WAR DIARY
or
INTELLIGENCE SUMMARY
(Erase heading not required.)

Army For

Hour, Date, Place	Summary of Events and Information	Remarks and references
Jan 27th ZEVECOTEN	Quiet day furnished R.E. fatigues. Gradually being reduced in numbers officers and men. Searles, Clarke, Murray gone to hospital. Thomson commanding.	
Jan 28th "	Last complete days rest. R.E. hut building fatigues again. Huts have to be built along hedges to deceive aeroplanes. Brigade conference on trenches.	
Jan 29th ZEVECOTEN to DICKIEBUSCH	Marched independently to LA CLYTTE and then as a brigade to Dickiebusch. A & B Coy under Partners to ELZENVALLE. Very disturbed night. A fire on the VIERSTRAAT road which could not be put out brought one company from their beds. Then about 10 violent firing in the direction of ST ELOI produced an order to stand to arms, which was cancelled in ½ an hour. It appears that Germans attacked in force and were badly mauled by French on our left.	
Jan 30th DICKEBUSCH to ELZENVALLE	Relieved P.P.C.L.I at ELZENVALLE; C Coy going to LA BRASSERIE. 2 close support but spent quiet night.	
Jan 31st ELZENVALLE trenches	7 to 10 relieved by companies starting about 8 pm in relief of Gloster Regt. Trenches far better than old ones. Distribution 2 coys firing line, 1 support, 1 regimental reserve.	

A P P E N D I C E S.

Bresserie
Bois Carré
Bois 40
Wytschaetebeek
Hollandscheshaar
St Eloi
Sketch of Trenches taken
over from French 31st Div by 27th Div
Scale
6th to 8th Jan 1915

88

VI

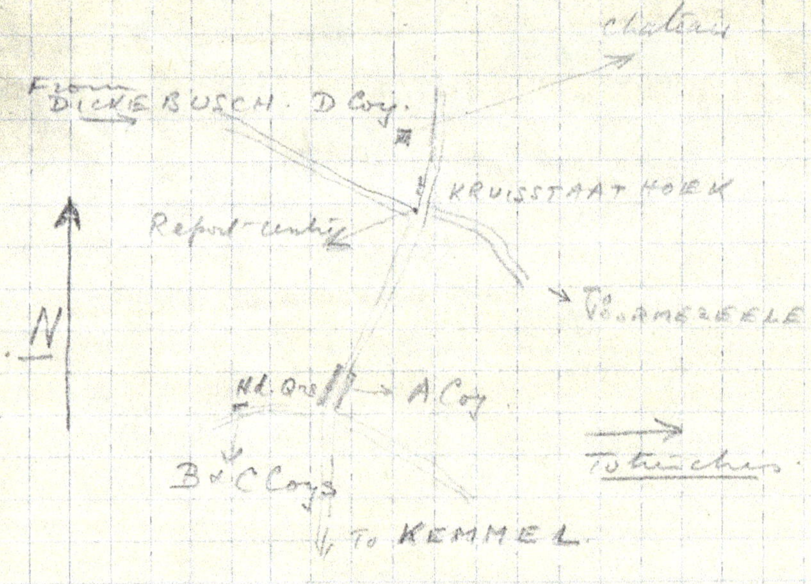

Rough sketch showing position of Battalion in support of remainder of 31st Brigade in trenches.

General scheme: 1 Brigade in trenches and close support
1 Brigade in brigade divisional support
1 Brigade in reserve
Two days in trenches

11.1.15.

ARB

1

Operation Orders

by

Lieut. Col. A.L. [illegible]

Comdg [illegible] Highlanders

Reference Trench Maps

[illegible]

1. The [illegible] Brigade will move to [illegible] [illegible] [illegible]

2. The Battalion [illegible] in close support of the trenches

3. The Battalion will parade at 7.30 pm in the following order of March

Headquarters

Machine Gun Section

'A' 'B' 'C' 'D' Companies in that order

A distance of 100x will be kept between 'A' Company and the Machine Gun Section and between all companies.

O.C. Companies will have an orderly

at the rear of each company to inform the next company directly there is a halt.

4. One limbered wagon per company one limbered wagon for Machine Gun and Headquarters, two water carts, two tool carts, tool carts and water carts to march in rear of Machine Gun Section Maltese cart will parade after water carts.

5. 100 rounds S.A.A. will be issued to each man in addition to the rounds already issued these extra rounds will be carried in bandoliers

6. Water bottles to be filled before parade

7. Lt. Ritchie and 2 cyclists will be at the cross roads in square H.29.B. by 7 pm. to receive a report from the Transport Officer the Cameron Highrs. and Gloucestershire Regt. when their respective transports has cleared the cross roads on its return to DICKEBUSCH. These reports will at once be sent to the C.O. by cyclists Orderly.

8. OC "D" Company will detail 1 officer and 20 men who will collect [illegible] from the Battalion [illegible] [illegible] [illegible] and [illegible] Regiment and transmit them to Brigade Headquarters by [illegible] [illegible]. Further instructions will be issued to this officer.

Sd. [illegible] Capt.
Adjt. [illegible] Highlanders

V3

81st Inf.Bde.

27th Div.

WAR DIARY

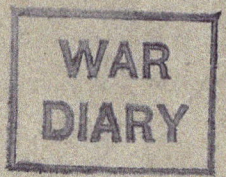

1st BATTN. THE ARGYLL & SUTHERLAND HIGHLANDERS.

F E B R U A R Y

1 9 1 5

1st Battalion The Argyll & Sutherland Highlanders.

February 1915

Feby 1st	Trenches	Lovely day. Battalion headquarters shelled pretty heavily at night. C Coy getting several men wounded. [Rations had to be taken up to trenches by night, which increases danger. Better also to have dressing station away from Hd Qrs.]
Feby 2nd.	Trenches to DICKEBUSCH	Both trenches and Batt. Hd Qrs shelled during day. Relieved by Gloster regt. in evening marching back by companies to DICKEBUSCH. [New and very scattered billets. Weather bad again] No deaths during tour of trenches. 13 men wounded.

1247 W 3299 200,000 (E) 8/14 J.B.C. & A. Forms/C. 2118/11.

Summaries are contained in F. S. Regs, Part II. and the Staff Manual respectively. Title pages will be prepared in manuscript.

INTELLIGENCE SUMMARY

(Erase heading not required.)

Hour, Date, Place		Summary of Events and Information	Remarks and references to Appendices
Feby 3rd	DICKEBUSCH	Quiet day in billets. [Men got hot bath at brewery on YPRES road. Germans shelled Batt. Hd Qrs – the first time they have shot at DICKEBUSCH] Capt Chrystal joined [Conference at Brigade Hd Qrs]	
Feby 4th	DICKEBUSCH to trenches	Started to relieve Glosters at 5 p.m. Firing line coys already had got into trenches when they received an order postponing relief as the Germans had broken through 28th Divisions line on our left. Battalion marched back W of BRASSERIE and waited. Very cold. Relief eventually carried out at 2 a.m., when 28th Division had reported all right. 2Lts Campbell and Robertson joined	
Feby 5th	Trenches	Fine day, Battalion Hd Qrs shelled in morning. Found working carrying parties and R.E. fatigues in evening. Casualties 2 men killed – [Ptes Laidlaw & Gilmour A Coy], 1 man wounded. [Both buried.]	
Feby 6th	Trenches	Urgent message to be ready to move at ½ hours notice cancelled. It appears that Germans had 150x of 28th Divisions trenches until this morning but were driven out by York & Lancaster Regt.	91st

1247 W 3299 200,000 (E) 8/14 J.B.C. & A. Forms/C. 2118/11.

Instructions regarding War Diaries and Intelligence Summaries are contained in F. S. Regs., Part II. and the Staff Manual respectively. Title pages will be prepared in manuscript.

INTELLIGENCE SUMMARY

(Erase heading not required.)

Hour, Date, Place	Summary of Events and Information	Remarks and references to Appendices
Feby 7th ELZONVALLE	Peaceful day. Nothing doing	
Feby 8th "	Aeroplanes busy all day and in afternoon billets badly shelled. Very good shooting. [1 room and kitchen knocked about. The M.O's primus stove, medical haversack, and three pairs of gum boots destroyed – luckily nothing was set on fire. vide appendix opposite] Relieved in evening by R. Scots, and proceeded to relieve Glosters in trenches. [New Battalion H.Qrs. dark but comfortable and not so liable to shell fire] Trenches in good order	// Notes on shell fire. Pallin had provided a haggis much appreciated by H.Qs night before. When report was sent in that our mess room had been shelled, following telephone message from staff captain was received "G.O.C. hopes mess plate and furniture were not badly damaged when mess room was ~~shelled~~ hit. R.A. were at once informed and have replied to place where they think fire was coming from. Good job you had the haggis yesterday." A reply as follows was sent. "Many thanks for kind enquiries – regret to report death from wounds of one primus stove, one surgical haversack, and three pairs of gum boots deeply regretted. R.I.P."
Feby 9th Trenches	Battalion reserve coy. shelled in their farm – fine day, aeroplanes busy, bombs dropped near Bn H.Q.	
Feby 10th Trenches DICKEBUSCH }	Relieved by K.S.L.I. Quick & good relief. Marched to hut shelters DICKEBUSCH very dirty and wet. Draft of 151 from 4th Bn waiting there. Two officers Grant and Campbell with them	
Feby 11th DICKEBUSCH ZEVECOTEN }	Marched in early afternoon to ZEVECOTEN. [Billetted in huts, and a few in houses]	
Feby 12th ZEVECOTEN	Brigadier inspected new draft. Very pleased – fine lot of old soldiers, if anything on the old side	
Feby 13th "	Wet day: C.O. inspected huts – comfortable but mud everywhere	
Feby 14th "	Wet day. Order to be ready to move at once, received at 4.30 pm, as trenches had been lost by 27th & 28th Divn S. of YPRES Canal. Marched off at 8.30 pm to DICKEBUSCH halting in bitter cold wind for some hours. Thence to halting place ¾ mile out of DICKEBUSCH where all men were squashed under cover. Very busy and disturbed night – artillery firing every second	
Feby 15th DICKEBUSCH	C & D Coys sent out to dig 2nd line of trenches already begun. After heavy shelling they were recalled, returning to halting place and remainder of Battn. to billets in DICKEBUSCH. C & D lucky to have no casualties. Busy day as orders were received to go to trenches in evening. Relieved D.C.L.I. and 60th on left section. Trenches very bad – New Battn. Hd Quarters only 200x from firing line, in dirty cellar 10' x 8'. No telephone communication with trenches. Quiet night – repairing trenches.	

Summaries are contained in F. S. Regs, Part II. and the Staff Manual respectively. Title pages will be prepared in manuscript.

INTELLIGENCE SUMMARY

(Erase heading not required.)

Hour, Date, Place	Summary of Events and Information	Remarks and references to Appendices
Feby 16th Trenches to DICKEBUSCH	Fairly quiet day. Some artillery fire. Relieved in evening by Glosters who changed their headquarters to VOORMEZEELE. Heavy firing about 9 pm soon quelled by artillery fire. Details of counter attack on night of 14/15th rather vague. It appears that Leinsters were driven or left their trenches. Germans (not in great strength) occupied them. First counter attack failed owing to C.O of Leinsters being shot while arranging it. D.C.L.I and KRR had little difficulty in regaining trenches. Some prisoners taken - very young and badly trained. In fact cold and damp worse enemies at present. Trenches bad. [L cpl. D. Graham A Coy, a fine soldier athlete and a very brave man shot dead. A loss to the battn.] Total killed 4. Good deal of firing on left in 28th Div area.	2 Lt Carr R E Capt Taylor - Leinsters 4 men of KRR buried by party - service read by adjutant. Place Hd Qrs farm.
Feby 17th DICKEBUSCH	Firing all night. Ordered to stand to at 11 a.m. as more trenches have been lost by 28th Div. Reinforcements arrived from LOCRE and BAILLEUL.	
Feby 18th DICKEBUSCH to trenches.	Relieved Gloster Regt in trenches. During the night a very gallant and useful reconnaissance was carried out by Captain Porteous who crawled out from trench 21 and gained much useful information about enemy's saps and parallel. He regained our own trenches safely. [Some excitement during the night as Captain Wilson reported from his trench that enemy were mining below him. The miner eventually appeared - a rat in the parapet.]	
Feby 19th trenches	C.S.M. Robb by a brave act brought back important information from No 19 trench in daylight when telephone communication had broken down. Capt. Porteous explained all the information he had gained overnight to G.O.C 82nd Bde at Bn Hqrs - received great praise. He attempted a further reconnaissance in the early morning but was compelled to return by snipers. Lieutenant R. Stirling shot through the head and instantly killed while bandaging a wounded man in trench 21	

91st

Instructions regarding War Diaries and Intelligence Summaries are contained in F. S. Regs., Part II. and the Staff Manual respectively. Title pages will be prepared in manuscript.

INTELLIGENCE SUMMARY

(Erase heading not required.)

Hour, Date, Place	Summary of Events and Information	Remarks and references to Appendices
Feby 20th Trenches & DICKEBUSCH	Fairly quiet day. SHELLY FARM where Capt Maclean and telephone operators were, shelled during day and set on fire by a flare ~~at night~~ in early morning – much S.A.A. destroyed. Relieved in evening by Glosta Regt and 1/7th Royal Scots in 19 and 20 trenches. H.Qrs and two coys returning to DICKEBUSCH – C Coy to VOORMEZEELE, D Coy to Chateau KRUISSTRAATHOEK. Major Kirk from 2nd Battn. waiting in DICKEBUSCH having come to command.	
Feby 21st DICKEBUSCH	Quiet day – fine and sunny – [Buried Lt Stirling and Lt Dunsmure of Cameron Highlanders at 3 p.m. Situation of reserved plot of ground for officers and men Highlanders Regts and Royal Scots – just E of DICKEBUSCH church on VIERSTRAAT road.] Major H.B. Kirk promoted to Bt Lt Colonel for services in the field.	
Feby 22nd DICKEBUSCH	[A & B Coys inspected by C.O in morning] Relieved Glosta Regt in trenches in evening. Fairly quiet night. Capt. Chrystal proceeded to join 2nd Battn.	
	Copy of letter from G.O.C. 27th Division to G.O.C. 81st Bde. The G.O.C. wishes to convey through you to Captain D.M. Porteous 1st Bn Argyll & Sutherland Highlanders, his appreciation of the excellent report (and sketch) of German trenches, forwarded under your No. 81/148 of the 20th instant. The report contains matter of great value and importance. The G.O.C. is well aware of the difficulties and dangers which must have been overcome by Captain Porteous in order to give such valuable information. Signed H.L. Reed Lt Col. G.S. 27th Divn dated 21st Feby 1915. Copy of memo. from G.O.C. 81st Bde to O.C. 1/A&S H. For your information and communication to Captain D.M. Porteous. Signed D.A. Macfarlane Bde Genl. Comdg 81st Bde dated 21.2.15.	

1247 W 3299 200,000 (E) 8/14 J.B.C. & A. Forms/C. 2118/11.

Instructions regarding War Diaries and Intelligence Summaries are contained in F. S. Regs., Part II. and the Staff Manual respectively. Title pages will be prepared in manuscript.

INTELLIGENCE SUMMARY

(Erase heading not required.)

Hour, Date, Place	Summary of Events and Information	Remarks and references to Appendices
Feby 22nd DICKEBUSCH to trenches	continued Copy of letter from 5th Corps to 27th Divn. Reference your G.S. 444 dated 21st Feby 1915 the Corps Commander has read the report on the reconnaissance carried out by Captain DM Porteous 1st Argyll & Sutherland Highlanders and appreciates the very good work done by this officer. Signed W. Robertson Major G.S. 5th Corps	
Feby 23rd Trenches	Quiet day – relieved firing line trenches. 2Lt H.B Campbell shot through the head and killed instantly. [A very brave and promising officer].	
Feby 24th Trenches to DICKEBUSCH	Trenches to DICKEBUSCH being relieved by Gloster Regt. Quiet day. Pioneers did good work making rifle racks, stands, trestles and planks for trenches, during this time.	
Feby 25th DICKEBUSCH	C.O inspected draft of 117 men under 2Lt Thorneycroft Mostly men left behind in India and returned men who were in hospital at Winchester. A fine draft. [Buried 2Lt HB Campbell in afternoon. Capt Fraser and Lt Nicholson buried at the same time.]	
Feby 26th DICKEBUSCH to trenches	Active measures against enemy's parallel and saps were to be undertaken, should clouds obscure moon. Firing line trenches strongly held by A & B Coys and 1 Machine gun with 1½ coys in close support by night. Bright moonlight prevented any possibility of an attack however. Bomb throwing assisted by advice from Captain Porteous, prevented enemy working openly in parallel opposite No: 19 trench. Divisional bomb throwers on the whole very indifferent and bombs failed to explode opposite No 21 trench. SHELLY FARM evacuated and new telephone exchange opened in WHITEHORSE CELLAR St. ELOI.	

9776

Instructions regarding War Diaries and Intelligence Summaries are contained in F. S. Regs., Part II. and the Staff Manual respectively. Title pages will be prepared in manuscript.

WAR DIARY
or
INTELLIGENCE SUMMARY
(Erase heading not required.)

Army Form C. 2118.

Hour, Date, Place		Summary of Events and Information	Remarks and references to Appendic
Feby 27th	Trenches to ZEVECOTEN	Marched back straight to rest area after relief by PPCLI. Relief well and quickly carried out. Casualties light. All ranks marched back very well. Billets and huts as before.	
Feby 28th	ZEVECOTEN	Day spent in cleaning up, made difficult by the filthy state of fields round the huts. 2/Lt Duff 4th Bn A&SH. joined with draft of returned hospital men. PPCLI reported in morning that a party of 35 had attacked german parallel, the night being cloudy and filled it in along a distance of 30–40x killing 16 Germans and taking 3 prisoners. Their own casualties fairly heavy. So ends a very strenuous month	

8 (k)

Reports on

Reconnaissances

File in 8 (B)

Copy

G X 240.

27th Division

Reference your G.S. 444 dated 21st Feb 15
The Corps Commander has read the report on the reconnaissance carried out by Captain D M PORTEOUS, 1st Argyll & Sutherland Highlanders, and appreciates the very good work done by this officer

W Robertson
Maj GS
5th Corps

21-2-15

Confidential

Headquarters,

5th. Corps.

I forward herewith a copy of a trench report of exceptional value, made by Captain D.M. Porteous, 1st.Bn.Argyle and Sutherland Highlanders on night of 18th/19th.February, 1915. which may be of interest to the G.O.C. 5th. Corps.

I have conveyed to this officer my appreciation of his good work under difficulty and danger, and his name is recorded amongst others for consideration as to submission for recognition on a future occasion.

T. D'O. Snow

21st.Feby.1915.

Major General.
Commanding 27th.Division.

GX 240

12.2 ?

V Corps
G.X. 238
21/2/15

Please say I have read this report & appreciate the very good work done by Captain Porteous.

[illegible]

Headquarters,

27th. Division.

I forward herewith a report of a reconnaissance carried out by Captain D.M.Porteous, 1st. Argyle and Sutherland Highlanders, on the night of the 18th/19th February, 1915, which contains valuable and interesting information which is of great service.

This reconnaissance was carried out in a bold and skilful manner by Captain Porteous at considerable personal risk, and I wish to bring his name to the favourable notice of the G.O.C. Division.

20th.February, 1915. Sd. D.Macfarlane, Br.General.

Commanding 81st.Infantry Brigade.

All reference to left or right of saps etc. refer to our own left or right.

---

1. Report on sap and parallel opposite No.21 Trench.

On the night of 18th/19th. I was asked to make a reconnaissance of the above.

The ground in the vicinity of No.21 Trench was new to me and I spent some time in getting the lie of our own trenches and the general position of the enemy's.

The latter was sniping a good deal and sending up many flares which made it very slow work. Before deciding on the possibility of making a successful attack it is most necessary to see the position by periscope by day, as crawling about by night does not always give you a good general impression of the lie of the ground.

Reference to attached map which does not pretend to more than general accuracy.

(1) Not knowing that A B was a raised road I took it to be a German Trench as my intentions were to find the left of the enemy's sap and parallel and if possible to get behind them on that flank I decided to crawl towards the apparent trench well to the left of the sap.

From the left corner of the left isolated redoubt of No.21 Trench a wet disused ditch or trench runs straight towards the German position. I worked throughout by myself having previously warned the men in No.21 and 22 trenches. I worked up close to the disused trench getting some lateral cover from the bank on the left of it. The raised road as it turned out to be, was about 50 yards from the point I started from and when some 10 yards off I decided that no one was there and got into a good position at the angle of the approach ditch and and the road where a few sand bags were built up and where there was a dip in the ground. The road was quite straight and offers a flat crest some 2 feet above the level of the fields.

3. In front of it on our side and to my right was a very open unoccupied flooded ditch. No one was opposite to me and I could not locate the German Trench beyond, as frequent flares went up and one would have easily seen over the straight skyline of the road.

I heard a good deal of talking, and as I thought, digging to my right front and beyond the road. I could not observe where the parallel, which was now to my right rear, was joined to the German Main Trench. I then crawled back, informed the O.C. No.21 trench of the nature of the supposed German Trench and crawled out to a point 10 yards from the left end of the German near papallel. It was some 20 yards away at most and as I could hear of no work in it I looked over at a low point in the parapet. It was unoccupied at that point and I crawled to the left end which turned in towards our line for 2 yards. The parallel appeared to run at a distance of some 20 yards from our No.21, to be heavily held on our right where the parapet is strongest and where it is very well protected by barbed wire "knife rests" On the left there is no wire as yet.

I dropped into the left end of the parallel and walked along it. It was about 1½ feet deep in water had some 5 to 5½ feet of cover, was 2 to 3 feet wide and traversed at intervals. I got to within what appeared to me about 15 yards from the occupied portion of the trench and then returned. I could hear people talking and reloading their rifles. I found a long handled spade near the left end, which I took back with me and decided to get back with what information I had and to see the position by day by periscope, before I went out again. Unfortunately there was no periscope available. I then walked along the line of trenches 19 to 23 and tried to get a rough bearing of the directions they faced in.

Between 2l and 20, I, in company with Lt. Campbell and Storlin walked to within 10 yards of the German Trench which was here about 50 yards from No. 20. They were firing hard but appeared unable to see us although we were up to their wire entahglement. They were shooting towards No. 19. I could not make out if this piece of trench was a second parallel, a main trench or a continuation of the big parallel I had first reconnoitred. The points that struck me about the German parallel was -

(i) My original position at corner of trench and road might be useful for a Machine Gun during a night attack but care would be needed not to fire into No. 19.

(2) An angular advance from our left covered by the fairly high parapet of the parallel and with bomb throwers working along inside of trench and possibly a Machine Gun in the German side of the trench might be successful. On the first hint of discovery a frontal attack might be pressed home at once as well.

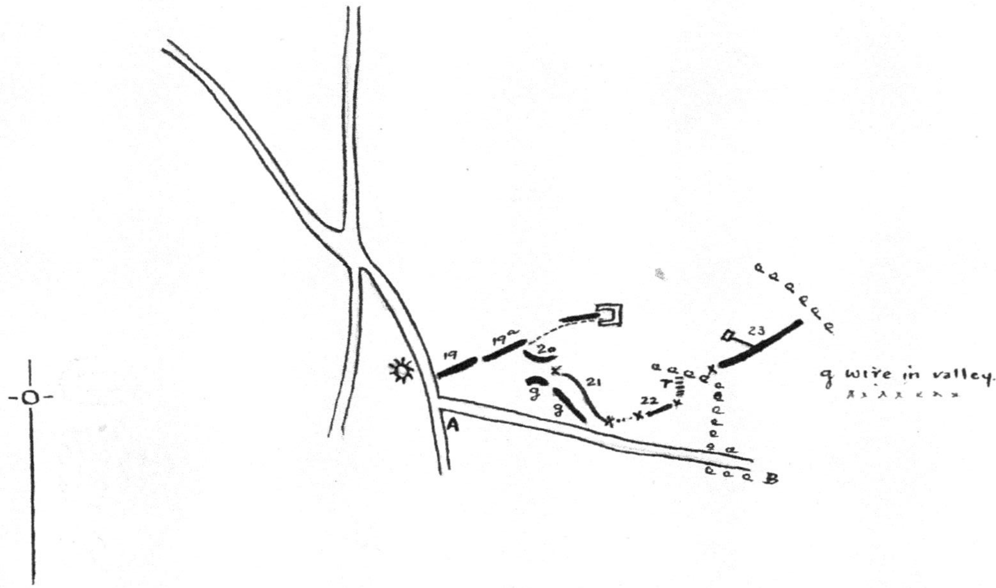

T ⁞ Old Dug-outs.

g. g. German Trenches or Parallels.

Road A. B. raised and shews straight Crest line.
Nearest point to our trench; left corner of 21
from about an old trench goes to road.
Parallel g g are 20 60x from 21.

!!

File in reconnaissance reports.

G X 459

G.b

G.S.329.

Headquarters,

5th. Corps.

The attached copy of a report on reconnaissance made by Lieut. G.D.G.Elton, Royal Irish Fusiliers, is forwarded for your information.

V. Baumgartner Major

for.

18th. March, 1915.

Major General.

Commanding 27th. Division.

7 20/III

Seen by BSSS

11 am

19.

Reconnaissance from BRICK KILN in front of

MOUND - 14-3-1915.

The lines marked on map attached are as nearly as possible the German trenches as observed.

The trenches in front of 18, 19, 20 and old 21 trenches appear very knocked about and the definite lines were hard to follow. They were very deep,in many cases, quite 7 feet deep.

Very little wire was observed all along the line. Just here and there were a few knife rests - evidently it had not been repaired after the bombardment.

Work could be seen here and there and then only consisting of bailing. Three excellent communication trenches ran back parallel with the St ELOI - WARNETON road. They connect with their main position along the ridge.

"A" appears to be a strong point built with sandbags.

"X - Y" is a long communicating trench with sandbags the whole length.

"B". At "B" there were a great many new sandbags which seemed to be laid out in a square, probably it is a strong point but the trees prevented me from seeing properly.

The Germans seen wore grey round hats with red bands. One man opposite 20 trench had a yellow band and one man further in rear had a helmet on.

One cannot see further East than a point in front of old 21 trench as the ground slopes down and is out of sight.

Sd. G.D G.Elton. Lt.

Royal Irish Fusiliers.

mi I.

V4

81st Inf.Bde.

27th Div.

WAR DIARY

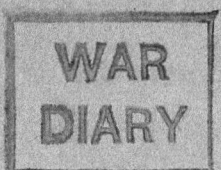

1st BATTN. THE ARGYLL & SUTHERLAND HIGHLANDERS.

M A R C H

1 9 1 5

1st Battalion The Argyll & Sutherland Highlanders.

March 1915

1st March	ZEVECOTEN	G.O.C. 81st Bde inspected draft. He was very pleased both with general appearance and turn out of the men. A very fine and welcome draft. C.O. inspected C & D Coys, whose turn out was good & handling of arms better than expected. "C" Coy very good. Companies engaged in making fascines and improving roads.
March 2nd	ZEVECOTEN	Very good work by Coys making knife rest entanglements, fascines etc and in improving paths to huts. Also under Coy officers for drill etc. All O.C. Coys expressed great satisfaction at men's steadiness and turn out.
March 3rd	ZEVECOTEN	G.O.C. 81st Bde and C.O. had an informal inspection of huts. Surroundings very dirty, making it difficult to keep huts clean or to dry clothes etc. Companies working as on previous days. Sick parade of 35 men. Nothing serious.

1247 W 3299 200,000 (E) 8/14 J.B.C. & A. Forms/C. 2118/11.

Instructions regarding War Diaries and Intelligence Summaries are contained in F. S. Regs., Part II. and the Staff Manual respectively. Title pages will be prepared in manuscript.

or

INTELLIGENCE SUMMARY

(Erase heading not required.)

Hour, Date, Place	Summary of Events and Information	Remarks and references to Appendices
March 4th ZEVECOTEN	Baths open all day for men. Much needed & appreciated as usual.	
March 5th ZEVECOTEN DICKEBUSCH	Marched in evening to DICKEBUSCH which was very congested with ammunition limbers, relieving infantry and Belgian artillery, and working parties all being in main street. Billets very scattered and bad. C Coy in close support to ELZENWALLE.	
March 6th DICKEBUSCH	Quiet day. Ordered to be prepared to move quickly as our artillery were bombarding enemy's advanced posts and trenches – our own trenches being vacated for this purpose and it was thought the enemy might retaliate by trying to rush our line. Bombardment lasted till 7 pm	
March 7th DICKEBUSCH trenches.	Marched in evening to relieve Gloster Regt in right sector Headquarters NEW FARM. Trenches dry and daily improving. Result of yesterdays bombardment seems to have been very slight!	
March 8th Trenches	Quiet day in trenches. Relieved firing line companies in evening – one company 9th A & S H. attached to A Coy in trenches 7, 8, S4 for instruction. Adjutant 9th ASH. Capt. Clive Gray came to NEW FARM to learn what he could. CO visited No. 8 trench with adjt & Captain Gray. Artillery firing star shells over HOLLANDSCHUR FARM made night rather noisy as everybody seemed to be letting off their rifles.	
March 9th Trenches to DICKEBUSCH	Relieved by Gloster Regt in evening after a quiet and peaceful two days. Casualties very light and after the St. ELOI section the new trenches were very comfortable and safe. Capt. MacLean returned from 8 days leave, probably our last "leave (and our first!) representative", as all leave has been stopped.	[illegible]

1247 W 3299 200,000 (E) 8/14 J.B.C. & A. Forms/C. 2118/11.

Instructions regarding War Diaries and Intelligence Summaries are contained in F. S. Regs., Part II. and the Staff Manual respectively. Title pages will be prepared in manuscript.

INTELLIGENCE SUMMARY

(Erase heading not required.)

Hour, Date, Place	Summary of Events and Information	Remarks and references to Appendices
March 10th DICKEBUSCH	Quiet day. News received of capture of NEUVE CHAPELLE and other successes.	
March 11th DICKEBUSCH trenches	Marched in evening to relieve Gloster regiment. [Relief quickly carried out except Machine gun which was delayed by an order miscarrying. A new M.O (temporary) Lt. Weir RAMC(T) attached to relieve Lt Selby who was wounded whilst on the road near HALLEBAST corner. His two orderlies, Ptes Munro and Gibb also both wounded - the latter dying of wounds in the evening. Lt Selby will be much missed as he was excellent with the men.]	
March 12th Trenches	Lovely spring day made very sad by death from wounds of Lt. J.C. Steel commanding D Coy. He was shot in the head while sitting in his dug out behind No 12 trench. It is not certain from which direction the bullet came. He lived, unconscious from 1.20pm to 7pm. X All trenches were ordered to open a rapid fire at 3pm to attract enemy's attention while an attack was made by 3rd Division. [Attack apparently failed]	
March 13th Trenches to DICKEBUSCH	After a fairly quiet day relieved from monotony by an order to repeat rapid fire as on previous day were relieved by Gloster Regt returning to DICKEBUSCH, leaving A Coy in ELZONVALLE.	
March 14th DICKEBUSH ELZONVALLE	Sunday, by now, recognised as a day of alarms fully maintained its reputation. A draft of 246 men from 3rd & 4th Battns - commanded by Lt Mackay with whom were Lts Thomas & Taylor arrived yesterday. Company strengths were equalised - becoming of quite respectable dimensions again. A Coy draft, however, their company being on detachment remained in DICKEBUSCH.	

Instructions regarding War Diaries and Intelligence Summaries are contained in F. S. Regs., Part II. and the Staff Manual respectively. Title pages will be prepared in manuscript.

or

INTELLIGENCE SUMMARY

(Erase heading not required.)

Hour, Date, Place	Summary of Events and Information	Remarks and references to Appendices
March 14th contained	Buried Lt Steel in afternoon beside Lts Stirling and Campbell. Capts. Maclwen, Boyle, Patten and 2Lt G I Campbell carrying the body. About 5-30 pm a violent cannonade was heard, and a particularly large explosion was heard and seen by some. Peaceful DICKEBUSCH became in a moment a pandemonium. Every battery in neighbourhood seemed to be firing or being fired at - a heavy rifle and machine gun fire was heard from St ELOI and soon ammunition limbers and horsemen were galloping down the street. Rumours were of course prevalent that trenches had been lost. The order to stand to was received and companies were ready to march at very short notice. The next order was to move to second line trenches in front of ELZONVALLE to which A Coy had already proceeded. Patrols of this coy had also gained touch with 80th Bde in VOORMEZEELE and Gloster Regt in NEWFARM - Lt GIBB doing good work. Companies ordered to march independently in order, C, D, B M.G. and draft of A Coy at five minutes interval. Move well carried out by all. C & D Coys were ordered to take on trenches on right of A Coy - B, draft of A Coy and M G kept as small reserve in ELZONVALLE. Trenches deepened and improved during the night. Camerons held trenches on our ~~left~~ right.	
March 15th	Headquarters were in chateau cellars. In early morning orders received to leave only 1 Coy in trenches retiring the other two to ELZONVALLE. Counter attacks had been partially successful only - the mound was held by the enemy - and our trenches on either side of it were untenable in consequence. Casualties in counter attacks very heavy. Battalion Hqrs was shelled all day but no casualties resulted. Orders received for men to eat emergency rations, as	

Instructions regarding War Diaries and Intelligence Summaries are contained in F. S. Regs., Part II. and the Staff Manual respectively. Title pages will be prepared in manuscript.

or

INTELLIGENCE SUMMARY

(Erase heading not required.)

Hour, Date, Place	Summary of Events and Information	Remarks and references to Appendices
March 15th continued	many men had no rations. Though shelling and rifle fire was heavy only 1 man was slightly wounded. In the evening proceeded to relieve Gloster Regt in trenches. A quiet night. Lt J O'Driscoll RAMC joined battalion.	
March 16th Trenches	No further news of yesterday's fight – "our line has been modified"! The mound partially blown away by mine partially by our shell fire. Enemy at one time held barricades in St ELOI. R E work on trenches at night.	
March 17th Trenches	A quiet day. Work on trenches under R.E supervision continued at night. Much useful work done – connecting isolated trenches etc. 1 Coy and 1 M.G of 9th A&S.H attached and did well	
March 18th Trenches	Usual day and night routine. Good work done, sniping from trenches at enemy working on their new line. Also artillery observation by Capt Young with successful results. In evening officers from Middlesex Regt 3rd Division came to visit trenches with a view to taking them over	
March 19th Trenches to DICKEBUSCH	Trenches 7, 7a, 8, 9, 10, ½54, ½55 handed over to Middlesex Regt. Remainder to Gloster Regt. Relief very slow – companies being very late reaching DICKEBUSCH. Billets there very scattered. B Coy with Camerons at ROZENHILL, A Coy HALLEBAST Farm, C & D Coys CANADA HUTS – but are very comfortable and well	

1247 W 3299 200,000 (E) 8/14 J.B.C. & A. Forms/C. 2118/11.

Instructions regarding War Diaries and Intelligence Summaries are contained in F. S. Regs., Part II. and the Staff Manual respectively. Title pages will be prepared in manuscript.

or

INTELLIGENCE SUMMARY

(Erase heading not required.)

Hour, Date, Place	Summary of Events and Information	Remarks and references to Appendices
March 20th DICKEBUSCH	Quiet day. Nothing to report. Men cleaning up and resting.	
March 21st DICKEBUSCH	A quiet Sunday for a change. Heard that we are to go to another area altogether. Change cannot be for the worse! Very sorry to hear Brigadier General D A Macfarlane D.S.O. has been relieved on account of age. His successor is Colonel Croker lately commanding Leicestershire Regt. In the morning C.O inspected draft which arrived on 14th. A fairly good lot. Some rather elderly – one too young. [Weather very good. Enemy shelled HALLEBAST CORNER in morning. In evening large fatigue parties under R.E supervision dug second line trenches etc.]	
March 22nd DICKEBUSCH	Quiet day. A weird instrument called a bomb catapult arrived and was tested with some success with sham bombs. Large fatigue parties again in the evening digging and wiring.	
March 23rd DICKEBUSCH	Catapult demonstration with live bombs in presence of Brigadier most successful. Whole battalion moved into CANADA HUTS which became rather crowded. Headquarters in small cottage near by. All officers live & sleep in 1 large hut not very waterproof. R E digging fatigues again in evening. Three men wounded.	
March 24th CANADA HUTS	Quiet day. Raining. More digging in evening.	
March 25th CANADA HUTS	Quiet day. Coys under Coy officers – much good work being done. No digging.	

or

INTELLIGENCE SUMMARY

(Erase heading not required.)

Instructions regarding War Diaries and Intelligence Summaries are contained in F. S. Regs., Part II. and the Staff Manual respectively. Title pages will be prepared in manuscript.

Hour, Date, Place	Summary of Events and Information	Remarks and references to Appendices
March 26th CANADA HUTS	As yesterday a quiet day. Bomb throwing classes range finding, company training etc. G.O.C. 27th Division came to see how we were in afternoon.	
March 27th CANADA HUTS	Captains MacIver, Wilson, Patten Jones, 4 Lts Gibb, Clarke, Thorneycroft, Campbell and 12 N.C.O went to ZEVECOTEN to pick up a motor bus en route for the new area which is now held by French IXth Corps. Brigadier inspected battalion lined up along several hedges to prevent aeroplane spotting them in the morning. Surely the first time the Battalion has had a generals inspection along hedge rows! Baths for some men in afternoon.	
March 28th CANADA HUTS	Corps commander General Sir Herbert Plumer arrived early in morning. Very pleased with the men he saw and state of huts. Remainder of battalion bathed. Digging parties in evening.	
March 29th CANADA HUTS	Fine cold weather continues. Party to French trenches returned – very pleased with new trenches. French very hospitable and did all they could to help. Digging parties again in evening.	
March 30th CANADA HUTS	Quiet day. Fears of possible Bismarck day (April 1st) attack. Whole 81st Bde reserve to 3rd Division.	
March 31st CANADA HUTS	Companies continue to work under Coy officers – bomb throwing – range takers etc busy. R.E. fatigue party again in evening.	

1247 W 3299 200,000 (E) 8/14 J.B.C. & A. Forms/C. 2118/11.

81st Inf.Bde.
27th Div.

1st BATTN. THE ARGYLL & SUTHERLAND HIGHLANDERS.

A P R I L

1 9 1 5

Original

Instructions regarding War Diaries and Intelligence Summaries are contained in F. S. Regs., Part II. and the Staff Manual respectively. Title pages will be prepared in manuscript.

WAR DIARY
or
~~INTELLIGENCE~~ SUMMARY
(Erase heading not required.)

Army Form C. 2118.

Hour, Date, Place	Summary of Events and Information	Remarks and references to Appendices
April 1st DICKEBUSCH	The battalion marched to ZEVECOTEN and with the remainder of the Brigade was inspected by G.O.C. 2nd Army. Sir Horace Smith Dorrien. After our rest men were able to get clean and looked well. The Brigade was drawn up facing RENINGHELST. A magnificent sunny spring day. The G.O.C. expressed to the C.O. his great satisfaction at the appearance and turn out of the men. After the inspection the Battalion marched home under the Sergeant Major, all officers and two N.C.O. per Coy. remaining on parade ground to be addressed by Sir Horace, whose speech was most interesting. He gave very high praise to the Brigade. "I have never seen such a fine body of men". Battalion order on subject attached. It was most gratifying to note the excellent appearance of men who had been many weeks in the greatest discomfort and of those who had only been in the country a few weeks and soldiers a few months. In this connection material of drafts remains excellent. Strength on parade was 808 all ranks. R.E. party to dig behind SPE LOI in evening.	
April 2nd DICKEBUSCH	Capt W. G. Neilson D.S.O arrived to join the Battalion early this morning. A quiet fine day. Nothing to report.	
April 3rd DICKEBUSCH	A conference at Brigade Headquarters ZEVECOTEN about new trenches to be occupied. Bomb throwing practice for all companies in the afternoon - followed by a football match officers v. sergeants. A draft under Lt. Lennox rejoined from BOSCHEPPE. Weather wet and stormy.	
April 4th DICKEBUSCH	Conference of officers commanding companies in the morning about new trenches to be occupied. Paraded 4 p.m. marched to YPRES (where a billetting party had gone in the morning) via	

W. R. Bogle Capt

.. 2/ Original

Instructions regarding War Diaries and Intelligence Summaries are contained in F. S. Regs., Part II. and the Staff Manual respectively. Title pages will be prepared in manuscript.

WAR DIARY
or
~~INTELLIGENCE SUMMARY~~
(Erase heading not required.)

Army Form C. 2118.

Hour, Date, Place	Summary of Events and Information	Remarks and references to Appendices
April 4th continued	OUDERDOM and VLAMERTINGHE. Men marched well and the battalion rested in famous Cloth Hall (or remains thereof) for two hours and then went out by trench parties to meet French guides just outside YPRES. A. B. C Coys and 4 M. Gs. in trenches D Coy and Headquarters in GLENCORSE WOOD in dug outs. The ~~of~~ relief very slow as roads were congested and the night dark. The French troops very kind and helpful in handing over. Difficulties in finding ones way among a maze of dug outs were great. Eventually the French commandant a most charming man and our interpreter Bazillon left about 3 a.m. the relief completed. Regiment relieved 68th, 114th, 9th Corps.	
April 5th Trenches.	Wet depressing day. Trenches and dug outs quagmires. A little shelling against B Coy trenches. Sergt Major Robb being badly hit. A great loss to the Battalion. Advance party of K.S.L.I. came in the evening to visit those trenches which we were to hand over to them on night 7/8th April.	
April 6th Trenches	A quiet day except for heavy shelling followed by rapid rifle fire against 69 trench and Cameron's left trenches, which lasted for a few minutes, causing support Coy to turn out and stand to arms. Trench parties of 9th R. Scots came to visit trenches which we hand over on night of 7/8th April. Continual change of trenches rather aggravating.	
April 7th Trenches	A quiet day. D Coy made new dug outs and cleaned old ones for B and C Coys who were relieved by K.S.L.I. late at night leaving only A Coy in fire trenches. Weather better, but still dull.	Col Capt

1247 W 3299 200,000 (E) 8/14 J.B.C. & A. Forms/C. 2118/11.

B' Original

Instructions regarding War Diaries and Intelligence Summaries are contained in F. S. Regs., Part II. and the Staff Manual respectively. Title pages will be prepared in manuscript.

WAR DIARY
or
~~INTELLIGENCE~~ SUMMARY
(Erase heading not required.)

Army Form C. 2118.

Hour, Date, Place	Summary of Events and Information	Remarks and references to Appendices
April 8th Trenches to YPRES	A quiet normal day. Relieved in evening by 9th R. Scots. Relief very late and billets not reached in YPRES till morning of 9th. B. C. D Coys left earlier and got into billets sooner. Head-quarters in a house in Rue des Chiens. Coys. in convent, rather crowded. Comparative luxury for all. Officers having beds wash-stands etc – things unknown for 6 months! During this four days tour the casualties were fairly heavy many occurring from shell fire – whizz bangs – the enemy opposite were careless and many were shot. The travelling cookers were brought to WESTHOEK and used for the first time in the trenches – but the "carry" was too far, and the food etc got cold. Indeed, the supply of rations and stores to trenches is a fine art, and here was badly run – causing unnecessary discomfort to all ranks. It is easy to lose ones way in a wood and carrying of trench rest employments and large boxes is slow and difficult. Also the roads from YPRES were very congested, being used by French and Canadian troops moving in relief. On left of 27th Division was 28th Division, Canadian Division and then Turcos.	
April 9th YPRES	A quiet peaceful day with only a few shells falling in the town. The men were confined to billets until boundaries were fixed. G.O.C 81st Bde visited billets occupied by Hqrs and C.O ~~those occupied~~ by men in the evening. Heard that Captain Poulton had been awarded the D.S.O.	

ARBoyle? Capt.

- 4 - Original

Instructions regarding War Diaries and Intelligence Summaries are contained in F. S. Regs., Part II. and the Staff Manual respectively. Title pages will be prepared in manuscript.

WAR DIARY
or
~~INTELLIGENCE SUMMARY~~

(Erase heading not required.)

Army Form C. 2118.

Hour, Date, Place	Summary of Events and Information	Remarks and references to Appendices
April 10th YPRES	C.O. inspected draft under Sergeant Johnstone (who had been left behind in 2nd?) A fine lot of men. A quiet day. Aeroplanes very active. Men allowed out in town. Aeroplanes very active.	
April 11th YPRES	A peaceful Sunday. Many aeroplanes about. The civil population of YPRES still seems large. The town is also teeming with troops of all sorts. A carrying fatigue party to HOOGE in the evening.	
April 12th YPRES to trenches	Marched from YPRES to new trenches previously inspected by company officers and N.C.O. Head quarters in BODMIN COPSE with 1 Coy in dugouts. Relief took some time and dawn now very early was on us almost before it was completed.	
April 13th Trenches	An average trench day. C.O. and G.O.C. 81st Bde visited 26 and 27 trenches, early morning. All trenches, breastworks and not very secure, besides having no firing step. Weather good.	
April 14th Trenches	Ordinary trench day. Enemy very quiet except for occasional shells and minenwerfer against C Coy which was very alarming and a new experience. Parapet badly smashed and one trench evacuated. When breach was made in parapet a machine gun was turned on to it and a few shrapnel. L cpl Simpson, Ptes Stewart, McMillan and Quinn C Coy all displayed great gallantry standing by Sgt. Constable in a "Johnson" hole during the day.	

C R Bagot Capt

5. Original

Instructions regarding War Diaries and Intelligence Summaries are contained in F. S. Regs., Part II. and the Staff Manual respectively. Title pages will be prepared in manuscript.

WAR DIARY
or
INTELLIGENCE SUMMARY
(Erase heading not required.)

Army Form C. 2118.

Hour, Date, Place	Summary of Events and Information	Remarks and references to Appendices
April 15th Trenches.	Quiet day, spent reconnoitring possible strong points, second line trenches, communication trenches. Occasional sniping but little else. C.O. nearly bagged. In the evening news received that enemy were going to attack. Agents [illegible] reported attack would take place 14th 15th or 16th. Enemy were going to use asphyxiating gases. Trenches were accordingly strengthened and extra S.A.A. sent down and barbed wire entanglements. The night however passed without incident.	
April 16th Trenches to SANCTUARY WOOD	Guides were sent to SANCTUARY WOOD by day so as to be able to lead companies to dug outs there in the evening on relief by Glosters. Relief rather slow and night dark. All companies and Hqrs in dug outs in close support of front line. About ½ mile from BODMIN COPSE just South of HOOGE on MENIN ROAD where Bde. Hqrs are situated. Brigade Hqrs are in cellar of chateau in which so many of the staff of the 1st Corps were killed during 1st battle of YPRES	
April 17th SANCTUARY WOOD	Company representatives practised with new bomb in the morning. An uneventful day. Many aeroplanes about. C.O. visited trenches round STIRLING CASTLE. New draft of 120 men under Lt. Muirhead and Newlands taken on strength. In evening carried rations and stores for Glosters and Royal Scots. Casualties for past 4 days been rather high being 47 killed and wounded.	[illegible signature]

1247 W 3299 200,000 (E) 8/14 J.B.C. & A. Forms/C. 2118/11.

6 Original

Instructions regarding War Diaries and Intelligence Summaries are contained in F. S. Regs., Part II. and the Staff Manual respectively. Title pages will be prepared in manuscript.

WAR DIARY
or
~~INTELLIGENCE SUMMARY~~
(Erase heading not required.)

Army Form C. 2118.

Hour, Date, Place	Summary of Events and Information	Remarks and references to Appendices
April 18th SANCTUARY WOOD	Three shells arrived early in SANCTUARY WOOD killing one man and wounding three. Overnight a mine had been exploded under crest of Hill 60 and the summit occupied. This seemed to enrage the enemy and he proceeded to shell YPRES and surrounding country with large and small guns. Our dug outs not very "healthy" stray bullets frequently coming quite close to H.qrs – indeed two men were wounded while making tea!	
April 19th SANCTUARY WOOD	A little shelling during the day but a good deal against YPRES. Second line trenches reconnoitred and dispositions if necessary decided upon. Companies under their officers practised fire control and attack formations. In the evening the MENIN ROAD was heavily shelled from the direction of GHELUVELT and owing to this rations were late in arriving. The transport in fact have a very perilous time in YPRES and beyond it and do their work well and without much praise. If anything the artillery fire grows more violent and SANCTUARY WOOD belies its name more every day.	
April 20th SANCTUARY WOOD	A bad day. In the afternoon about 4 p.m. began the fiercest bombardment the battalion has yet met. From Hill 60 now held by our troops to the trenches E of HOOGE the enemy literally plastered the the countryside with every sort of shell. YPRES itself was devastated with 17 inch shells and every inch of country seemed to be covered with smoke and lead! Many shells gave off, on	A R Bagshaw

1247 W 3299 200,000 (E) 8/14 J.B.C. & A. Forms/C. 2118/11.

7; Original

WAR DIARY
or
~~INTELLIGENCE SUMMARY~~

(Erase heading not required.)

Army Form C. 2118.

Instructions regarding War Diaries and Intelligence Summaries are contained in F. S. Regs., Part II. and the Staff Manual respectively. Title pages will be prepared in manuscript.

Hour, Date, Place	Summary of Events and Information	Remarks and references to Appendices
April 20th (continued)	explosion foul fumes which made the eyes water and the throat rough. All ranks went underground at once and casualties were few. Telephone wires were at once rendered useless, and orderlies carrying messages had a dangerous & exciting duty. Sergeant Yeansley and L.cpl Maclean did fine work mending broken wires. The relief of trenches was delayed as the carts could not move along the MENIN road. However eventually, they arrived at midnight and the lengthy issue of double rations began, after which companies already detailed moved off to relieve the Glosters. Trenches held as follows. A Coy C1, C2, C3 – "C" Coy C4, C5, D Coy C6 C7 C8, C9. B Coy in BODMIN COPSE. Relief was completed before dawn with few casualties. companies working well and in complete accord with Gloster Regt as usual. The endless shelling of Hill 60 and YPRES continued	
April 21st Trenches	Much shell fire all day and a minenwerfer very active against our right trenches. Little damage done, and the men behaved excellently but the effects are certainly nerve shattering. Lt McCutcheon rather shaken but controlled his platoon well under shrapnel and machine gun fire. The method employed by the enemy with his minenwerfer was as follows – A few small bursts of machine gun fire along the top of the parapet to range his gun – then a minenwerfer (the shell of which can be seen coming), then a few rounds shrapnel, a machine gun directed against the gap in the parapet and also at the top of the other parapets to catch heads looking over.	A R Boyle Capt

1247 W 3299 200,000 (E) 8/14 J.B.C. & A. Forms/C. 2118/11.

8. Original

Instructions regarding War Diaries and Intelligence Summaries are contained in F. S. Regs., Part II. and the Staff Manual respectively. Title pages will be prepared in manuscript.

WAR DIARY
or
~~INTELLIGENCE~~ SUMMARY
(Erase heading not required.)

Army Form C. 2118.

Hour, Date, Place	Summary of Events and Information	Remarks and references to Appendices
April 21st (continued)	During the night frequent bursts of rapid fire machine gun fire and shrapnel made the trenches and BODMIN COPSE very unhealthy. Our artillery, however, soon silenced the enemy, who did not seem anxious to leave his trenches.	
April 22nd Trenches	Enemy continued to show much activity against our trenches in spite of our artillery firing ~~against~~ on their trenches. In the afternoon and evening heavy firing to the North made us wonder what was happening. Later rumours came through that the line had been broken, the Turcos having fled; and that the enemy were on the line WIELTJE – BOESINGHE. A disturbed night with news anything but good though still vague. Rumours plentiful. No doubt that poisonous gases had been used and that the Turcos had run away.	
April 23rd Trenches.	More rumours and some confirmation of the retreat of the Turcos. The Canadian Division had been left with its left flank exposed had swung round and fought and driven back the Germans. In the morning two trenches of the 28th Division had been assailed but were at once retaken by the East Surrey Regiment. Situation regarded as bad but troops are being hurried up. Orders in case of a retirement issued to C.O. and afterwards to companies, should a re-adjustment become necessary. Companies in fire trenches report that enemy's troops opposite them have weakened, and that their position is only lightly held except for Machine Guns of which there are many. Enemy are still using five minute bursts of fire, which are quite ineffective and useless and are not replied to by our troops.	

A R Boyle Capt

1247 W 3299 200,000 (E) 8/14 J.B.C. & A. Forms/C. 2118/11.

9. original

Instructions regarding War Diaries and Intelligence Summaries are contained in F. S. Regs., Part II. and the Staff Manual respectively. Title pages will be prepared in manuscript.

WAR DIARY
or
~~INTELLIGENCE~~ SUMMARY
(Erase heading not required.)

Army Form C. 2118.

Hour, Date, Place	Summary of Events and Information	Remarks and references to Appendices
April 24th Trenches.	News scarce and indifferent. Little activity on our front but the battery supporting us has been ordered to turn two of its guns round and fire to the North! Minnenwerfer (christened "Minnie"!) active until stopped by a few H.E. shells, Capt. Portions doing observation officer. Men have now no fear of this form of explosive. News received in evening more re-assuring - many fresh troops have arrived and we are to fight. About 1500 enemy troops observed massing behind hill near ZANDVOORDE and it was thought a demonstration would take place. But nothing out of the ordinary happened. Weather fine and aeroplanes very busy.	
April 25th Trenches	Minnenwerfer again busy! also many H.E. shells against our trenches on the right. One Machine gun blown on to the air but not damaged at all - the shell which caused this did not explode but penetrated the parapet, throwing sandbags out one of which broke Pte Friggs back. It then lay in the trench and was buried carefully by the R.E. team. On the spot Huns fire very bad and much damage should have resulted. Buried Friggs in the evening; burial interrupted by a perfect hail of bullets which caused everybody to lie down by the grave.	
April 26th Trenches.	Combined attack by Lahore Division and some French troops made only fair progress. Message from Sir John French states that the enemy's offensive was broken, that the tide had turned and that enemy was in small numbers and tired.	
April 27th Trenches	The unwelcome attentions of the minnenwerfer again directed against C2 and C3 trenches but good practice by howitzers with Capt. Portions observing the results of shots silenced it. As a retaliation all our trenches shelled in afternoon and evening.	A R Bigh Capt

1247 W 3299 200,000 (E) 8/14 J.B.C. & A. Forms/C. 2118/11.

10 Original

Instructions regarding War Diaries and Intelligence Summaries are contained in F. S. Regs., Part II. and the Staff Manual respectively. Title pages will be prepared in manuscript.

WAR DIARY
or
~~INTELLIGENCE SUMMARY~~
(Erase heading not required.)

Army Form C. 2118.

Hour, Date, Place	Summary of Events and Information	Remarks and references to Appendices
April 28th Trenches.	Much shelling all day, but no attack. An anxious 24 hours. A draft of 60 O.R. arrived and were divided amongst companies and sent to join them. Much good work done on all trenches which were made better in every way. All men working well.	
April 29th Trenches	A fairly quiet day with occasional bursts of shell fire. Minenwerfer silent, and great hopes entertained that it was knocked out by the Howitzers. The [illegible] however who had taken over our left trench C4 received the unwelcome attentions of another further along the line. C.O. visited Brigade to discuss plans should withdrawal become necessary. The salient has now become so pronounced that one is literally fired at from three sides, and undoubtedly it would be an advantage to flatten the salient.	
April 30th Trenches.	A quiet day in front of us, but sounds of very heavy fighting to our left and rear. French attack North near PILCKEM made progress, but news still very scanty. April ends with the probability of a withdrawal to a new line. Men in good spirits if rather tired. Casualties fairly heavy, but enemy much weaker in front and his trenches (very strong) are lightly held.	

[signature] Capt.

1247 W 3299 200,000 (E) 8/14 J.B.C. & A. Forms/C. 2118/11.

81st Inf.Bde.
27th Div.

WAR
DIARY

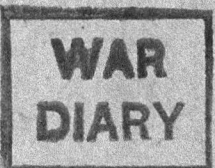

1st BATTN. THE ARGYLL & SUTHERLAND HIGHLANDERS.

M A Y

1 9 1 5

WAR DIARY
or
INTELLIGENCE SUMMARY
(Erase heading not required.)

Army Form C. 2118.

Instructions regarding War Diaries and Intelligence Summaries are contained in F. S. Regs., Part II. and the Staff Manual respectively. Title pages will be prepared in manuscript.

Hour, Date, Place	Summary of Events and Information	Remarks and references to Appendices
May 1st Trenches	Quiet day. Heavy shelling by field guns against D Coy's trenches but little effect. Nothing to report.	
May 2nd Trenches	Fairly quiet night and day. Preparations for withdrawal [such as removing trench stores, spare S.A.A. bombs to SANCTUARY WOOD.] Enemy undoubtedly weaker in our front. This apparent from volume of fire and patrols reports.	
May 3rd Trenches	Day spent removing remaining stores etc from BODMIN COPSE and trenches before withdrawal [which was ordered for the evening. New line of trenches in SANCTUARY WOOD was perfected by a[illegible] [illegible] line good but not complete.] In the evening trenches evacuated – Two parties leaving from each trench, the first at 10.30 p – the second at midnight. Two men with flare pistols were left in each trench to deceive the enemy and a patrol under Lt. Neill was left in front of BODMIN COPSE to ascertain when enemy discovered our withdrawal. B Coy and 1 platoon of D Coy were ordered to take up part of new line as 9th R. Scots were ordered North to assist 28th Division if necessary. Withdrawal admirably carried out by all companies. Night dark and rainy. Lt. Neill's patrol gained touch with enemy about 6 a.m. May 4th.	A R Bot[illegible] Capt

Instructions regarding War Diaries and Intelligence Summaries are contained in F. S. Regs., Part II. and the Staff Manual respectively. Title pages will be prepared in manuscript.

WAR DIARY
or
INTELLIGENCE SUMMARY
(Erase heading not required.)

Hour, Date, Place	Summary of Events and Information	Remarks and references to Appendices
May 4th Trenches	After a miserable early morning in bivouacs when it rained hard it faired about 10.30 a.m. Companies in second line trenches were shelled fairly heavily. 9th R. Scots took over our portion of trenches at 3 p.m. Relief quick and simple. Germans in no place nearer than 200 yards from our line.	
May 5th Trenches.	SANCTUARY WOOD Built dug outs for men and officers all day. Working parties in evening constructing strong points and helping R.E. Fairly quiet day.	
May 6th Trenches.	Continued work on dug outs as yesterday. Quiet day.	
May 7th Trenches	Quiet day with a little shelling. Companies in formed dug outs as day before. A definite plan of dug outs was fixed. Every company had artillery trenches (i.e. narrow deep ones) to use in case of shelling. Exits to dug outs large and alarm post fixed. This should always be practised.	
May 8th Trenches	A hard cruel day. The Germans began shelling trenches in front line about 6 a.m. Bombardment terrific. About 10 a.m. battalion was ordered to proceed to West of BELLEWAARDE LAKE, gain touch with P.P.C.L.I. who had been shelled out of their front line trenches, and restore the situation! A patrol under Lt. Gibb preceded the battalion. Companies ~~moved~~ in the following order, crossing MENIN ROAD	A R B[illegible]

1247 W 3299 200,000 (E) 8/14 J.B.C. & A. Forms/C. 2118/11.

Army Form C. 2118.

Instructions regarding War Diaries and Intelligence Summaries are contained in F. S. Regs., Part II. and the Staff Manual respectively. Title pages will be prepared in manuscript.

WAR DIARY
or
INTELLIGENCE SUMMARY
(Erase heading not required.)

Hour, Date, Place	Summary of Events and Information	Remarks and references to Appendices
May 8th (continued)	at the double, and with five minutes interval between coys: Heavy shelling continued, but luckily there were no casualties. A Coy proceeded to E chussett, S of BELLE WAARDE FARM. Headquarters and remainder halted in wood square I 11 D. It was very hard to obtain information either about general situation, the position of the P.P.C.L.I or the whereabouts of the 80th Brigade Headquarters under whose orders the Battalion now was. However Lt Gibb by excellent work [during which L/Cpl Park (a brave and promising corporal) was killed] found P.P.C.L.I and gained a general idea of the situation. About the same time two 80th Bde orderlies were intercepted and then a message with two of our own orderlies was sent back to 80th Bde. From information gained it seemed that the 28th Division had given way, and that the enemy were advancing down the railway and North of it. It was decided, therefore, to send one Company (D) to RAILWAY WOOD to deny this important position to the enemy. This was done, and soon afterwards B Coy was sent to assist and orders were given that trenches should be dug to strengthen the position and at the same time keep touch with the K.S.L.I who were on the left of P.P.C.L.I. [While attending a wounded man Lt. Clarke was hit in the head by a shrapnel bullet.] Orders were soon after received that a complete line of trenches from I 11 B to I 7 A was to be constructed. Accordingly A & C Coys	A R Bo[illegible] Capt

WAR DIARY
or
INTELLIGENCE SUMMARY
(Erase heading not required.)

Army Form C. 2118.

Instructions regarding War Diaries and Intelligence Summaries are contained in F. S. Regs., Part II. and the Staff Manual respectively. Title pages will be prepared in manuscript.

Hour, Date, Place	Summary of Events and Information	Remarks and references to Appendices
May 8th continued	were ordered to prolong B Coys line to the right. Tools were scarce and work was not very far advanced when orders were received to stop work, as 28th Division was going to counter attack North of railway and the Battalion was to co-operate and retake P.P.C.L.I. trenches S of railway. Work was stopped, companies were ordered to concentrate at I 11 B although no definite orders as to time or nature of the counter attack had been given. Patrols were just starting to reconnoitre ground to be covered when a message was received stating that the proposed counter attack had already taken place and been successful. Instead, therefore, of attacking, we were ordered to fill the gap between P.P.C.L.I. and "successful" 28th Division. A and D Coys were sent off under Capt. Neilson to do this. Shortly after their departure an officer of the Middlesex Regt when questioned stated that the counter attack had failed entirely. This was confirmed by Capt Neilson and the 80th Bde informed to that effect. Orders were then received to withdraw to G.H.Q. line, and hold that portion of the line between POTIZJE and the MENIN ROAD. This order was however, cancelled and the battalion ordered to occupy the trenches to S of MENIN ROAD which was done by 4 a.m. on May 9th.	A R Boyle Capt

1247 W 3299 200,000 (E) 8/14 J.B.C. & A. Forms/C. 2118/11.

Army Form C. 2118.

Instructions regarding War Diaries and Intelligence Summaries are contained in F. S. Regs., Part II. and the Staff Manual respectively. Title pages will be prepared in manuscript.

WAR DIARY
or
INTELLIGENCE SUMMARY

(Erase heading not required.)

Hour, Date, Place	Summary of Events and Information	Remarks and references to Appendices
May 9th Trenches	During the morning we were shelled but men were able to get some cooking done and a little sleep. About 2.30pm a very heavy bombardment of firing line trenches especially those held by K.S.L.I began, and in a few hours time the order was received to send two companies to RAILWAY WOOD, I 11 B, to support K.S.L.I. A and D Coys were soon on their way, moving across country to avoid the shelled avenues, and followed by C.O. and adjutant with 4 signallers. At RAILWAY WOOD no definite information was obtained for some time from K.S.L.I and nothing was done, as the enemy seemed to make no progress. About 5.30pm Captain Porteous D.S.O was mortally wounded by a stray bullet while visiting one of his platoons. About 8pm an officer came to HQrs from the front line and reported on the situation. The bombardment had been very heavy and our trench which was badly sited had suffered severely. The enemy however after one advance to our line had shown no inclination to repeat what must have been a very costly move. It is interesting to note, that men were seen wearing kilts, khaki trousers and even French uniforms – indeed an officer of the K.S.L.I shot a German Highlander with his own rifle. A full sketch and a proposed plan of action was sent to 80th Bde ~~[illegible]~~	[illegible]

Instructions regarding War Diaries and Intelligence Summaries are contained in F. S. Regs., Part II. and the Staff Manual respectively. Title pages will be prepared in manuscript.

Army Form C. 2118.

WAR DIARY or INTELLIGENCE SUMMARY

(Erase heading not required.)

Hour, Date, Place	Summary of Events and Information	Remarks and references to Appendices
May 9th trenches	for approval. G.O.C. 80th Bde soon came himself and approved of proposed dispositions, thanking C.O. for excellent information. The badly damaged trench referred to above was ordered to be repaired by D Coy, held by whole Company during the night and lightly held during the day following. As it was probable owing to its bad siting the trench would be shelled on the next day, a supporting trench correctly sited was started by ½ A Coy and a certain amount of progress made. The night passed fairly quietly. An enemy's working party working on a trench some 60 yards from that now held by D Coy and calling themselves K.O.Y.L.I. were badly mauled by rapid fire opened by one of our patrols, causing much waste of S.A.A. on their part.	
May 10th trenches	At daylight O.C. D Coy manned the dangerous trench above referred to after effecting all repairs possible, with 2½ platoons withdrawing remainder under Lt. McNaught to RAILWAY WOOD, where A Coy under Lt Gibb were also kept. Shelling started early, the morning's aeroplanes being very active. From 6 am to night fall a torrent of shells rained on the fire trenches N of MENIN ROAD and South of Railway and on the intervening country between them and the G.H.Q. line. The trench occupied by D Coy, received	[illegible] Capt

1247 W 3299 200,000 (E) 8/14 J.B.C. & A. Forms/C. 2118/11.

Instructions regarding War Diaries and Intelligence Summaries are contained in F. S. Regs., Part II. and the Staff Manual respectively. Title pages will be prepared in manuscript.

or

INTELLIGENCE SUMMARY

(Erase heading not required.)

Hour, Date, Place	Summary of Events and Information	Remarks and references to Appendices
May 10th continued	a terrific hammering and the C.O. decided to withdraw the garrison. This was done in a very efficient way by Lt Mackay, who was the last to leave the trench. Casualties were fairly heavy. Soon after this by intercepting two orderlies of 4th K.R.R. who were on their way to 80th Bde Hqrs it was learnt that the front line trenches were practically destroyed. The C.O. therefore decided to send up A Coy at once to support 4th K.R.R. and 4th R.B. if required, and at the same time send a patrol to get in touch with the Hqrs of each of these battalions. B and C Coys in the G.H.Q. line were at the same time warned to be ready to move at a moment's notice. Soon after this it was seen that men of 4th K.R.R. and 4th R.B. were leaving their trenches and the situation looked ugly. B and C Coys were accordingly ordered to advance from G.H.Q. line and support A Coy now in the wood I 11 D. Just before leaving A/C.S. Sgt Major W. Johnstone was killed by a shell. The advance of B & C Coys across an area of a mile in depth which was swept with shell fire was magnificently carried out. Casualties were surprisingly few, which was due to the excellent formation of each company. Not a moment was lost and discipline was perfect. It was a most inspiring sight. B Coy was at once ordered to move up in support of A Coy and ½ C Coy was soon sent to assist B Coy. Thus at about 2 p.m. the situation was as follows: Hqrs ½ C Coy D Coy and 2 M guns were at RAILWAY WOOD and A Coy was supporting 4th K.R.R. and R.B. while B Coy and ½ C with 2 M guns were held in local	

Instructions regarding War Diaries and Intelligence Summaries are contained in F. S. Regs., Part II. and the Staff Manual respectively. Title pages will be prepared in manuscript.

or

INTELLIGENCE SUMMARY

(Erase heading not required.)

Hour, Date, Place	Summary of Events and Information	Remarks and references to Appendices
May 10th continued	reserve ready to counter attack if enemy should advance and break the line. On proceeding to his position with his guns Capt. Patten was wounded. While leading his platoon to wood in I11 D Lt. Neill collected and reformed 150 men of 80th Bde who were running away, and led them up with his platoon. About this time 2/Lt Gibb was killed instantly by a shell whilst gallantly reconnoitring the position. No definite news, however reached Hqrs until Lt Bolton who had been sent forward by O.C. B Coy sent back an excellent report on the situation and from it the C.O was able to report the situation to the 80th Brigade. This information at once produced an order to counter attack and re-capture lost trenches. The Commanding Officers of the 4th K.R.R. and R.B deemed a counter attack impossible. The remainder of these two Battalions were holding a line called the cavalry line which ran about 100 yards E of Hooge Chateau to which place C.O decided went so as to confer with C.Os of 4th K.R.R & R.B. There, the opinion was arrived at that any chance of the counter attack succeeding was negatived by the insufficient artillery support and the state of the wood in front of the trenches – the trees forming a natural and almost insurmountable abattis as they lay after being pulled by shells. The 80th Bde agreed and ordered a new line of trenches to be dug between the line now held and the German line. Work on new line to be covered by a covering party from 1st A & S Highlanders. This plan was however	[signature] Capt

Instructions regarding War Diaries and Intelligence Summaries are contained in F. S. Regs., Part II. and the Staff Manual respectively. Title pages will be prepared in manuscript.

or

INTELLIGENCE SUMMARY

(Erase heading not required.)

Hour, Date, Place	Summary of Events and Information	Remarks and references to Appendices
May 10th continued	given up as it would have been impossible to make any useful form of trench in the time at our disposal. The final orders were to the effect that the line now held was to be held at all costs — 1st A&SH to relieve part of 2nd Camerons Hdqrs in trenches and join on to 4th K.R.R. 50 yards N. of MENIN Road. This part of the line — i.e. from BELLEWAARDE LAKE to SANCTUARY WOOD was held by 4th R.B., 4th K.R.R., 1st A&SH, 2nd Camerons — and was placed under command of Lt Col J Campbell comdg. 2nd Camerons. X	
May 11th trenches	A and B Coys were detailed to hold our portion and after reconnoitring it, these companies occupied it before dawn. The other two companies were placed as follows — D Coy still attached to K.S.L.I. 80th Bde. C Coy in support in chateau garden HOOGE. M. guns 2 covering MENIN Road 1 with B Coy 1 in reserve. There was much difficulty in getting rations issued and firing line companies were without any.	
May 12th Trenches	Early morning of May 11th found Hqrs in chateau HOOGE with companies disposed as above. About 8 a.m. a runner from B Coy reported enemy were heavily shelling B Coys' trenches and using gas, and that O.C. B Coy had ordered trenches to be evacuated. Headquarters at once left HOOGE chateau and occupied a deep trench at back of chateau garden. When here it was reported by Camerons that Lt Col Campbell was wounded (about 9 a.m.) and that the command of the line devolved upon Lt Col Kirk. A fuller report on attack of enemy against B Coy trenches was, apparently, received about this time both from O.C. B Coy and O.C. 2nd Camerons who were on right of B Coy.	[illegible]

1247 W 3299 200,000 (E) 8/14 J.B.C. & A. Forms/C. 2118/11.

Instructions regarding War Diaries and Intelligence Summaries are contained in F. S. Regs., Part II. and the Staff Manual respectively. Title pages will be prepared in manuscript.

INTELLIGENCE SUMMARY

(Erase heading not required.)

Hour, Date, Place	Summary of Events and Information	Remarks and references to Appendices
May 11th continued	It appeared that after shelling and bombing B Coy's trench with every form of projectile for a long time the trench became untenable in places and some of the garrison were ordered to withdraw to a communication trench in rear. The trench being manned by very few rifles and 1 M.G. under Capt Young. Soon afterwards the enemy were seen to be advancing and occupied the trench to our right; gas was also released but not in great quantities and did no damage. Soon after this Captain Young saw the enemy advancing up a communication trench and being also under enfilade fire ordered the few men he had with him to retire. This was done, the M.G. firing to the last minute and having, unfortunately, to be abandoned in the trench. The M.G. team and Capt Young being the last to retire. Orders were issued at once to O.C. B Coy and Cameron Highlanders that the trench was to be retaken. This was done almost immediately the enemy putting up no fight at all. From this time (10.30 a.m.) onwards the fighting was spasmodic but fierce. The enemy continued to show activity against that part of the line to the E edge of SANCTUARY WOOD and though frequently offering a good target both for Machine guns and rifles never showed any inclination to advance with any dash. Owing, however, mainly to the very winding nature of the trenches, he frequently could enfilade our trenches should he succeed in capturing another bit to the right of our line. O.C. B Coy reported at 3.30 pm that he had again been forced to evacuate trenches which he had retaken in the morning, but stated he was counter attacking at once. This was done but also being unsupported on its right and Lt Neill in charge of it having been severely wounded as the line advanced, the attack failed.	[illegible] Capt

1247 W 3299 200,000 (E) 8/14 J.B.C. & A. Forms/C. 2118/11.

Instructions regarding War Diaries and Intelligence Summaries are contained in F. S. Regs., Part II. and the Staff Manual respectively. Title pages will be prepared in manuscript.

INTELLIGENCE SUMMARY

(Erase heading not required.)

Hour, Date, Place	Summary of Events and Information	Remarks and references to Appendices
May 11th continued	The Germans however showed no desire and the ground fought for was eventually held by neither side. At night fall, the front line trenches were held by A & B Coys and part of C with the remainder of C in support. D Coy remaining at I 11 B with K.S.L.I. All ranks had shown great endurance during the day's fighting the majority fighting without rations and water. Casualties on the whole few. 2Lt Neill and Lt Rollow both wounded in the afternoon, Capt Young was left alone with B Coy. 2Lt McCutcheon commanded A Coy being the only officer with it. C Coy had Capts Wilson, 2Lts Robertson and Henderson and D Coy ~~Capt~~ Lt Mackay and 2Lt McNaught. Rifle shooting was bad and more enemy should have been bagged, but the men showed splendid spirit. A In the evening Headquarters stayed in trench dug out just S of MENIN Road where they had gone at about 1.30pm and shared a large underground warren with Cameron Hgrs. [Several congratulatory messages and telegrams received from various generals and good news of French advance near Carency.	
May 12th Trenches	Beyond occasional sniping and a few shells the day passed quietly. The enemy frequently offered a good target and many were killed or wounded. After the terrible din and terrific fire of previous days it seemed as if the offensive was stopped. D Coy who had ~~[illegible]~~ held trench sited and dug by A Coy on night of 9th/10th ~~[illegible]~~ without casualty (thus paying a compliment to the designer) rejoined and were placed in support in trenches in chateau garden. 2Lt McNaught injured by a Jack Johnson explosion. The night passed quiet by but on	

1247 W 3299 200,000 (E) 8/14 J.B.C. & A. Forms/C. 2118/11.

[signature]

Instructions regarding War Diaries and Intelligence Summaries are contained in F. S. Regs., Part II. and the Staff Manual respectively. Title pages will be prepared in manuscript.

INTELLIGENCE SUMMARY

(Erase heading not required.)

Hour, Date, Place	Summary of Events and Information	Remarks and references to Appendices
May 13th trenches	began a terrific bombardment at 4 a.m., which lasted all day, chiefly directed against front line trenches N. of MENIN road and at the West end of HOOGE village where Hqrs dug out was. The trenches occupied by the battalion escaped attention. News was scanty as all telephone wires were cut. It was learnt however, that the cavalry had been driven from their trenches by the extremely heavy bombardment. At one time, it afterwards transpired the enemy were nearly ~~of~~ abreast of RAILWAY WOOD North of the railway. The cavalry in the evening by a very gallant but costly counter attack, retook lost trenches and the situation became normal. In the evening a platoon of the 5th D.L.I. Infantry was attached to each of our companies in the firing line and support. Major Ernor 5th D.L.I. commanded attached company. Lt Thorneycroft rejoined and took over command of A Coy	
May 14th trenches	A quiet day. Our own guns are asserting themselves. Nothing of interest to report, and casualties very light.	
May 15th trenches	Again a quiet day with news of a relief in the near future. Never was news so welcome. Work on trench improvement continued.	
May 16th trenches	A strangely quiet Sunday. A draft of 138 men under 2/Lt Gunn arrived in the evening and ~~were~~ were sent to ZOUAVE WOOD. Nothing of interest to report. Work on improving trenches continued	A.K. Boyle capt

Instructions regarding War Diaries and Intelligence Summaries are contained in F. S. Regs., Part II. and the Staff Manual respectively. Title pages will be prepared in manuscript.

INTELLIGENCE SUMMARY

(Erase heading not required.)

Hour, Date, Place	Summary of Events and Information	Remarks and references to Appendices
May 17th Trenches	A quiet day with a few whizz bangs going over our dug outs, trenches and down the MENIN ROAD. In the evening officers of the 2nd Cavalry Brigade came to look over trenches which they were to relieve the following night. Nothing else to report.	
May 18th Trenches	In the evening, after a peaceful rainy day, the long looked for relief arrived, in the shape of the 19th Hussars. The actual relief was much delayed owing to two of the attached 5th D.L.I. platoons getting lost. They were found however just as dawn was breaking on the following morning.	
May 19th trenches to bivouacs near BASSE BOOM.	Headquarters were the last to leave [the famous and demolished village of] HOOGE. [[illegible] and a few men were left to act as guides and mentors to the cavalry.] The battalion marched [back down the MENIN Road through the ruins of YPRES which (if many generals and congratulatory messages are to be believed) it had helped save from the enemy! -] to VLAMERTINGHE [where hot tea was waiting for officers and men. The march was resumed as a battalion to bivouacs about 1 mile N of HEASKEN near divisional Hqrs at BASSE BOOM where we arrived at 8.45 am. The battalion marched out of YPRES on April 12th and had been under fire in trenches or dugouts for 36 days – very nearly a	[illegible]

Instructions regarding War Diaries and Intelligence Summaries are contained in F. S. Regs., Part II. and the Staff Manual respectively. Title pages will be prepared in manuscript.

INTELLIGENCE SUMMARY

(Erase heading not required.)

Hour, Date, Place	Summary of Events and Information	Remarks and references to Appendices
May 19th continued	a record. On the march back, very few men fell out, although a great many had not removed their boots since April 12th. In the afternoon G.O.C 2nd Army General Sir H. Plumer visited the bivouacs informally and expressed to the C.O his great appreciation of the work done by the Battalion. Application for leave for all officers now serving with the battalion who had landed with it in December was submitted. Maj Genl. Sir David Henderson R.F.C. came to visit the battalion in the evening with Major Clarke G.S.O 2 27th Division. Names of officers who marched out from YPRES on evening 12th April as follows. Lt. Col H.B Kirk (commanding) Capt. W.G. Neilson 2nd in command. A Coy Capt. Porteous Lt Thorneycroft, Gibb, McCutcheon B Coy. Capt Young Lts. Clarke Bolton, Neill C Coy Capt Wilson, Lts Robertson, Henderson, Duff, Kincaid Lennox D Coy Capt Maclaren, Lts Mackay, Campbell, Taylor, McNaught Adjutant Captain A.R. Boyle. Transport Officer 2Lt S. Rome Qr. Mr. Lt J. Heatly. Sergt. Major Gilmour. M.G. Officer Capt Patten Joined Battalion between 12th April – 19th May. 2Lts Newlands Muirhead, Gunn, Grant Killed Capt Porteous, Lt Clarke 2Lt Gibb Wounded Capt Patten, 2Lt Taylor, Muirhead, Neill Lt Bolton, 2Lt Newlands, McNaught. Sick ~~ltt~~ Capt Maclaren, Lt Thorneycroft, Duff, Kincaid Lennox, Campbell, Grant, Marched from line 19th May Lt Col H.B KIRK Capt W.G. NEILSON Capt. Adjt A.R. BOYLE, Capts WILSON, YOUNG, Lts MACKAY 2Lts ROBERTSON HENDERSON, Thorneycroft, Gunn, [illegible] McCutcheon (absent on escort duty 4 days) Those in printed letters never having left battalion.	A draft under 2Lt Berry awaited the battalion.

A.R. Boyle Capt

Instructions regarding War Diaries and Intelligence Summaries are contained in F. S. Regs., Part II. and the Staff Manual respectively. Title pages will be prepared in manuscript.

INTELLIGENCE SUMMARY

(Erase heading not required.)

Hour, Date, Place	Summary of Events and Information	Remarks and references to Appendices
May 20th Bivouacs	News was received early that the Field Marshal commanding in chief would inspect the battalion at 12 noon. All ranks laboured to get shaved and as clean as possible, no easy matter after so many days away. Parade in fatigue dress - coats, kilts without aprons, no arms or equipment. Glosters, Camerons and 1/A&SH drawn up in hollow square. A very eulogistic speech was made by Sir J French who thanked all ranks for the part they had taken. He also stated that the Germans had endeavoured to capture YPRES with the idea of impressing Italy who was hesitating to join the allies. By our gallant defence (the 27th Division) we had enabled Italy to decide to join the allies, and that very day she would sign the necessary declaration. Three cheers were given for the Field Marshal, and the troops returned to bivouacs. Capts Wilson, Boyle, Young and Lt McCutcheon left for England on leave till 26th. Lt O'Driscoll accompanying them. Lt J. Cunningham joined the battalion and posted to B. Coy.	
May 21st Bivouacs	Baths in RENINGHELST available [for the use of the battalion greatly appreciated. Otherwise an uneventful day.] C.O. inspected 3 drafts which had arrived since middle of April. A fine lot of men well equipped. Major Elphinstone joined and became 2nd in command.	
May 22nd Bivouacs	C.O. inspected transport and horses and found all in good order. The part played by 2nd Lt Rome, Sgt Smith and the transport during the fighting was no light one, and was admirably performed. The MENIN road and YPRES were continually under shell fire and yet every night rations and stores were brought up.	A R Boyle Capt

1247 W 3299 200,000 (E) 8/14 J.B.C. & A. Forms/C. 2118/11.

Instructions regarding War Diaries and Intelligence Summaries are contained in F. S. Regs., Part II. and the Staff Manual respectively. Title pages will be prepared in manuscript.

or

INTELLIGENCE SUMMARY

(Erase heading not required.)

Hour, Date, Place	Summary of Events and Information	Remarks and references to Appendices
May 23rd [illegible]	Lt Greenfield rejoined after a short time with the 3rd Battalion. [G.O.C. 81st Infy. Bde having gone on leave Lt-Col [illegible] assumed command of the Brigade. A quiet day	
May 24th [illegible] to support	Lt. Ritchie rejoined from 3rd Batt. 2Lt G. I. Campbell also returned from ROUEN. 2Lt Pursley joined battalion. During early hours of the morning the enemy launched a strong "gas attack" against trenches E. of YPRES and with much shell fire tried to capture front line of trenches. The gas was used in unprecedented quantities and was felt many miles from the firing line. The Battalion was ordered to "stand to" and be ready to move at half an hours notice. Eventually it was ordered to march at 3.45 pm to Huts H 11 C to support front line if necessary. [A return to the neighbourhood of YPRES was anything but popular! Brigade Hqrs to H 16 A. No use was made of the battalion however, and the night passed quietly.]	
May 25th Huts H11C	A quiet day. Stayed in huts all day. [A few shells from the N.E. and aeroplanes active. Otherwise nothing to report]	
May 26th Huts H11C	Again a quiet day with nothing to report.	
May 27th Huts H11C	Officers rejoined from leave in early morning. A quiet day. C.O. returned from 81st Bde Hqrs in evening. Orders received in evening to march in the morning 28th May to billets near LOCRE on our way South. YPRES burning fiercely in the evening lit up the sky for miles round.	

Instructions regarding War Diaries and Intelligence Summaries are contained in F. S. Regs., Part II. and the Staff Manual respectively. Title pages will be prepared in manuscript.

~~WAR DIARY~~ or INTELLIGENCE SUMMARY

(Erase heading not required.)

Hour, Date, Place	Summary of Events and Information	Remarks and references to Appendices
~~WITH THIRD CORPS~~		
May 28th HILL to LOCRE	Paraded 6 a.m. Marched [via VLAMERTINGHE and OUDERDOM] to ZEVECOTEN where draft under Captain Forbes, Capt. Cooper and 2Lt Scott met the battalion. Thence to huts and bivouacs in DRANOUTRE [1 mile beyond LOCRE arriving about 11 a.m.] Men marched very well.	Map Sheet 36.1/40000
May 29th LOCRE to LE PETIT MORTIER	An early start marching as a Brigade to BAILLEUL, 1st A&SH leading. General Pulteney commanding 3rd Corps inspected the Brigade as it marched past him just outside BAILLEUL. He praised the battalion, remarking "a fine body of men." Reached billets [in a small pretty village] near STEENWERCK [called LE PETIT MORTIER] square G 3 B sheet 36 1/40000. The first time since January that we had been as a battalion in France itself, and all glad to be away from Belgium. [In the afternoon representatives from each company and HQrs went to look over new trenches at present held by the Buffs – going by motor bus to ARMENTIÈRES. Their reports on return were very favourable.] 2Lts Rodgers, Gillespie and Nielson joined being posted to D, A and B Coys respectively. In the evening Lt Col Mackenzie M.V.O., Major Tweedie, Captains Campbell (adjt), Lumsden and Walker all of 10th Battalion rode over to see us. We also received a message by orderly from 2nd Batt. A historic village now – LE PETIT MORTIER!!	[signature] Capt

1247 W 3299 200,000 (E) 8/14 J.B.C. & A. Forms/C. 2118/11.

INTELLIGENCE SUMMARY

(Erase heading not required.)

Hour, Date, Place	Summary of Events and Information	Remarks and references to Appendices
May 30th LE PETIT MORTIER to trenches I.21.A	Marched at 1.30 p.m – [after orderly room and a voluntary church parade held by Rev. Gilchrist, and headed by pipes and drums of 10th Battalion on our way] to ARMENTIÈRES. Lt. Col Mackenzie M.V.O., and Major Tweedie and Capt Campbell with many old 91st N.C.O. now with 10th Battalion came to say goodbye. Capt Muir also came earlier in the morning.] The battalion halted in a field at ERQUINGHEM LYS H.5.A from 4 pm – 7 pm – [Captain Purves and Lt & QrMr Clayton 2nd Battalion came to see us. The pipers of 2nd Battn. played us into ARMENTIÈRES in the evening.] Took over trenches in Squares I.21.A and B from Buffs. Relief quick and simple. In the trenches on our right were the 2nd Battalion. And so, at about midnight of 30th/31st May the two battalions for the first time in the history of the regiment fought and found themselves side by side! The night passed quietly. Lt Col Gore, Major Hyslop and Capt. Kennedy visited HQrs soon after relief.	
May 31st Trenches	The trenches consisted of breastworks, strong and well-built but had rather too many dugouts and shelters. Would be very unpleasant in a heavy bombardment. The lines of the 2nd Battalion were even more luxurious – flower gardens, garden seats and summer houses being frequent! Heard in the afternoon that we were to relieve 3rd R.B. in trenches in front of CHAPELLE D'ARMENTIÈRES the following day. C.O. and adjt proceeded to inspect this line at once. HQrs CHAPELLE D'ARMENTIÈRES in a house near the cemetery. Communication trenches good. A very quiet day	A.C. Boyle Capt

V5

81st Inf.Bde.
27th Div.

WAR DIARY

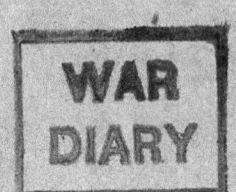

1st BATTN. THE ARGYLL & SUTHERLAND HIGHLANDERS.

J U N E

1 9 1 5

Original

Instructions regarding War Diaries and Intelligence Summaries are contained in F. S. Regs., Part II. and the Staff Manual respectively. Title pages will be prepared in manuscript.

1.

WAR DIARY
or
INTELLIGENCE SUMMARY
(Erase heading not required.)

Army Form C. 2118.

Hour, Date, Place	Summary of Events and Information	Remarks and references to Appendices
June 1st Trenches RUE DE BOIS 7.I.21	A quiet day. G.O.C. 22nd Division visited trenches and saw enemy's trenches through a periscope, probably for the first time. Men were allowed to visit 2nd Battn trenches - and vice versâ. In evening moved to relieve 3rd R.B in trenches square I 10 and 1 coy of 1st R. Scots. Relief without incident - quick and no casualties. Hqrs CHAPELLE D'ARMENTIÈRES.	Sheet 36 1/40,000 map. France
June 2nd Trenches I 10.	A quiet day. Brig. Genl. Carter, Capt Holland, O.C. and adjt of 9th R. Scots visited trenches in morning. Nothing of any interest to note. Trenches need a good deal of work on them, as there are weak places. A second line must also be dug, as support at present are practically in fire trenches. Excellent communication trenches from Hqrs to all trenches. The amount of sandbags and wood used in making this line and the communicating trenches would have been most useful at ST ELOI!	
June 3rd. Trenches	All quiet as usual. New scheme of holding our other trenches nearer RUE DE BOIS working alternately with Ulster Regt discussed [illegible]. Work on trenches undertaken - heightening parapets - making m.g. positions - cutting grass (with bayonets as no sickles available). Sanitation a most important matter now. Germans announced fall of PRZEMYSL by large placards hung in front of their parapet.	[illegible] Capt

1247 W 3299 200,000 (E) 8/14 J.B.C. & A. Forms/C. 2118/11.

Original 2

Instructions regarding War Diaries and Intelligence Summaries are contained in F. S. Regs., Part II. and the Staff Manual respectively. Title pages will be prepared in manuscript.

WAR DIARY
or
INTELLIGENCE SUMMARY
(Erase heading not required.)

Army Form C. 2118.

Hour, Date, Place	Summary of Events and Information	Remarks and references to Appendices
June 4th Trenches	All quiet as usual. Scheme for new trench line to be taken over discussed at Bde Hqrs by adjt Glosters. C/A&SH. Bde Major sick. Usual work in trenches. Great improvements being made everywhere.	
June 5th Trenches	Nothing of any interest. A shell or an aeroplane or even a bullet is almost longed for to break the monotony. Heavy fighting at SOUCHEZ can be heard all day long.	
June 6th Trenches	Spy hunted in the evening as light had been reported.	
	Nothing to report in the way of war! C.O and adjt visited Glosters Hqrs in orchard and arranged future relief and dispositions, incidentally getting sniped while looking at new 2nd line – quite refreshing reminding one of St Eloi.	
	2Lt P.N Peel arrived with draft of 100 men.	
June 7th Trenches	C.O and adjt went to Bde Hqrs and again had a bullet pass between them! Enemy showing a little more activity but 2Lt McCutcheon and his snipers seemed to keep them down. 9th R. Scots who take over two left sections of our line and 4th R Scots who will take over the right sections came to visit trenches. At night much more activity. M. guns and rifles busy firing one thing or proving that a new [illegible] specimens of Hun was opposite – or else that the line was being stunned. The C.O inspected the draft. A poor lot of men.	A R Boyle Capt

1247 W 3299 200,000 (E) 8/14 J.B.C. & A. Forms/C. 2118/11.

Original 3

Instructions regarding War Diaries and Intelligence Summaries are contained in F. S. Regs., Part II. and the Staff Manual respectively. Title pages will be prepared in manuscript.

WAR DIARY
or
INTELLIGENCE SUMMARY
(Erase heading not required.)

Army Form C. 2118.

Hour, Date, Place	Summary of Events and Information	Remarks and references to Appendices
June 8th Trenches to Billets	A quiet day. G.O.C. 8th I. Bde and Major A.L. [illegible] Clark visited the trenches. Thundery weather with some rain. In evening 9th R. Scots relieved 72, 71 sections and [illegible] R. Scots 70 and 69 sections. Relief quick with exception of Machine gun. Lt. St. Clair reported arrived to join 1st Bn after recovery from wound. A Coy to second G.H.Q. line – remainder to billets – ARMENTIÈRES.	
June 9th ARMENTIÈRES	Officers billetted in various houses all large and comfortable. Hqrs 4, Rue Nationale where all officers messed, luxury such as this unknown since leaving England. B. C. D Coys billetted – HOSPICE CIVIL. All very comfortable. Coys sold beer in billets which was appreciated. Only 30 % of men allowed out in town. The last draft drilled and inspected by adjutant. Turning out much better. General appearance of battalion very dirty, this being the first opportunity for cleaning up.	
June 10th Billets	Companies at disposal of company officers route marching and drilling. A quiet day. Officers of the battalion who had been in Malta dined together i.e. Col. [illegible] Capts [illegible] [illegible] Boyle [illegible] Lt [illegible]	
June 11th Billets	Officers of 1st Bn lunched with officers of 2nd Bn. and a historic photograph was taken afterwards at 6 Rue de Strasbourg. All regular officers of both battalions being taken. Present on this occasion were Lt Col [illegible]	A.R. Boyle Capt

1247 W 3299 200,000 (E) 8/14 J.B.C. & A. Forms/C. 2118/11.

Original 4.

Instructions regarding War Diaries and Intelligence Summaries are contained in F. S. Regs., Part II. and the Staff Manual respectively. Title pages will be prepared in manuscript.

WAR DIARY
or
INTELLIGENCE SUMMARY
(Erase heading not required.)

Army Form C. 2118.

Hour, Date, Place	Summary of Events and Information	Remarks and references to Appendices
June 11th continued	Major Elphinstone, Capts Forbes, Cowper, Wilson, Boyle (adjt), Young, Lts Mackay, St Clair, Cunningham, Ritchie, Greenfield, Robertson, 2/Lts Campbell, Purdey, Rowe, Maclean, McCutcheon. Lt & QrMr J. Heatly. Many new faces but all very pleased to meet for the first time. 2Lt Wood 7th Worcestershire Regt (T) attached to adjutant this day for instruction	
June 12th billets trenches	Relieved Glosster Regt. in trenches 63 – 66 both inclusive in the evening. Trenches good – with broad communication trenches. Companies in alphabetical order from the right. Headquarters in dug out built by Gloster Regt in an orchard I 15 c. Relief well and quickly carried out. A quiet night.	
June 13th trenches	A Sunday with its usual bad luck. A Minenwerfer shell landed in 65 trench and killed L. Cpl Lees and Pte Formby wounding 6 others. Another disaster which might have had serious consequences also occurred. The Hqrs dug out began making ominous noises, and one cross beam was seen to be splitting. While trying to prop up the roof the cross beam suddenly broke and the whole roof fell in. Colonel Mck Lamp nearly buried and having his head bruised badly. It was a lucky escape. Furniture was damaged and meals had to be taken in the open air.	A R Boyle Capt

1247 W 3299 200,000 (E) 8/14 J.B.C. & A. Forms/C. 2118/11.

Original 5.

Instructions regarding War Diaries and Intelligence Summaries are contained in F. S. Regs., Part II. and the Staff Manual respectively. Title pages will be prepared in manuscript.

WAR DIARY
or
INTELLIGENCE SUMMARY
(Erase heading not required.)

Army Form C. 2118.

Hour, Date, Place	Summary of Events and Information	Remarks and references to Appendices
June 16th trenches	Capt. Cooper reported a mine being actively worked by the enemy quite close to his advanced trench in 66 section. His expert miners in D Coy were positive that sounds were heard. A mining expert from R.E. Mining company was called for. Otherwise the day was uneventful. The weather keeping fine and hot.	
June 17th trenches	Expert from R.E. Mining. Company confirmed the presence of enemy's mine near advanced trench in front of 66. A boring was made and blue clay located - which is easy soil to work in. G.O.C. 8th I.B. visited trenches and informed us that 67 was to be taken over as well as present line - an extra company of the Glosters being used for this purpose. In the evening 1 Coy Glosters took over 67 from Camerons. A practice gas alarm was attempted but failed owing to gas gongs not being sufficiently noisy and sentries not obeying orders laid down. The use of gas by the Germans has not only caused much pain to those who inhale it but a perfect trail of correspondence on the use and abuse of every sort of respirator. The present pattern is a smoke helmet with talc or film eyepiece, each man carries also a respirator of cotton waste covered with gauze - the waste being soaked in a special solution. Bottles of this solution at frequent intervals and vermorel sprays are also kept in the trenches.	[illegible] Capt

1247 W 3299 200,000 (E) 8/14 J.B.C. & A. Forms/C. 2118/11.

Original 6

Instructions regarding War Diaries and Intelligence Summaries are contained in F. S. Regs., Part II. and the Staff Manual respectively. Title pages will be prepared in manuscript.

WAR DIARY
or
INTELLIGENCE SUMMARY.
(Erase heading not required.)

Army Form C. 2118.

Hour, Date, Place	Summary of Events and Information	Remarks and references to Appendices
June 18th trenches	Waterloo day passed quietly - and with the exception of a few shells nothing out of the ordinary occurred. Relief in the evening quickly and easily effected. For the first time we relieved from each end of the line held by us simultaneously. The result was successful. A & D coys returned to ARMENTIÈRES B to trench 67, C to FARM X and support line. The arrangement of 2 coys permanently out is rather trying.	
June 19th billets	Baths for 140 men of A Coy, who had not been back into billets since arrival in this part of the line was very welcome. A Field General Court Martial tried Ptes Ross (absence) and Canday (absence) in the morning. Adjutant prosecuted. Lt St Clair and Capt Forbes members. This was the first case of one of this battalion being tried by F.G.C.M since battalion landed. Lt Col Gore and Capt Kennedy to Lens	
June 20th	A quiet peaceful day. Church parade in billets. Lt Purdey visited Bde Hqrs having been reported unfit on account of defective eyesight. Baths for those who had not had them. Lt Woods left trenches on bath	C R Boyle Capt

(73989) W4141—463. 400,000. 9/14. H.&J.Ltd. Forms/C. 2118/10.

Original 7.

Instructions regarding War Diaries and Intelligence Summaries are contained in F. S. Regs., Part II. and the Staff Manual respectively. Title pages will be prepared in manuscript.

WAR DIARY
or
INTELLIGENCE SUMMARY.
(Erase heading not required.)

Army Form C. 2118.

Hour, Date, Place	Summary of Events and Information	Remarks and references to Appendices
June 21st billets	Sentences on Ptes Ross & Cardey promulgated. Pte Ross convicted absence and disobedience of orders 3 years penal servitude commuted to 2 years I.H.L. Pte Cardey convicted of absence 1 year imprisonment commuted to 84 days F.P. No I. In the afternoon transport vehicles and horses inspected by A.S.C. inspecting officer who expressed satisfaction of the turn out and condition of horses. Saddlery was [illegible] however. A & D Coys marched to relieve B & C respectively in the [illegible]	
June 22nd billets	A quiet day. B & C Coys bathed. Behaviour of men in the town considering their long enforced absence from any form of comfort very good. Leave now open to 8 [illegible] O & men per battalion per week	
June 23rd billets	A quiet day nothing to report of any sort	
June 24th billets trenches	The papers of June 23rd publish long extract from London gazette of 22nd inst "mentioned and recommended for gallant and distinguished service in the field" Major (Bt Lt Col) H.B. Kerr, Capt & Adjt A.R. Boyle, Capt C.H. Pattin, Capt D.M. Parsons D.S.O. (K in A), Capt J.H. Young, 2nd Lt R. Gibb (K in A), L/Cpl Arnuit (No 6..)	A R Boyle Capt

Original 8

Instructions regarding War Diaries and Intelligence Summaries are contained in F. S. Regs., Part II. and the Staff Manual respectively. Title pages will be prepared in manuscript.

WAR DIARY
or
INTELLIGENCE SUMMARY.
(*Erase heading not required.*)

Army Form C. 2118.

Hour, Date, Place	Summary of Events and Information	Remarks and references to Appendices
June 24th (continued)	Pte Cleary (No. 10651), Pte Gray (No: 606) Pte Stead (No 50) Previous to this Sergt Yeansley, Bandsm Counter Pte Lambie, C.S.M. Robb, L-cpl Sinclair had been awarded D.C.M. for gallant & distinguished work from Dec 1914 to April 1915. The last two (Robb & Sinclair) being unfortunately killed during that time. In evening relieved Gloster Regt in trenches and again the relief was very quietly completed. A message received at about 10.30 pm stated that Capt & adjt A R Boyle and Capt J H Young had been awarded the Military Cross.	
June 25th trenches	A quiet day nothing to report. Rev Gilchrist visited trenches. No news of enemy [illegible].	Extract from London Gazette dated War Off. June 23rd. H.M. the King has been graciously pleased to approve of the undermentioned honours and rewards for distinguished service in the field with effect from June 3rd inclusive. Capt A R Boyle, [illegible] J H Young
June 26th trenches	A further and different disposition of trenches announced today. The Battalion and Glosters working alternately to take over trenches 60 – 63 both inclusive 64 trench to be held by 9th R Scots – 65, 66, 67 trenches to be taken over by Camerons and 1st R Scots working alternately. O.C. and adjt 9th R Scots came to discuss this relief. A quiet day enemy active at night.	

A R Boyle Capt

Original 9

Instructions regarding War Diaries and Intelligence Summaries are contained in F. S. Regs., Part II. and the Staff Manual respectively. Title pages will be prepared in manuscript.

WAR DIARY
or
INTELLIGENCE SUMMARY.
(Erase heading not required.)

Army Form C. 2118.

Hour, Date, Place	Summary of Events and Information	Remarks and references to Appendices
June 27th trenches	Sunday again bright & hot. 2nd Lt [illegible] Campbell about 1.15 a.m. went out without warning his company commander or the companies on either side of his own, and either losing his way or running [illegible] hastily because he had seen an enemy patrol was shot by B Coy listening post sentries. A waste of a very valuable life. He was a gallant & promising officer. Buried in CHAPELLE D'ARMENTIERES at 2.30 pm by Rev Gilchrist. In the evening we relieved 2nd Batt. A & S H. in trenches 60, 61, 62 and support trenches. Disposition of coys now as follows. A, B, C Coys in 60, 61, 62 respectively. D Coy in support trenches scattered about, 1 Coy Glosters in 63, 1 Coy Glosters in G.H.Q. line. Relief quick & well carried out. A strange thing for one battalion to relieve another in the same regiment.	
June 28th trenches	A showery, windy day. The C.O. and adjt. of Glosters went round trenches in afternoon. The line on the right (i.e. 60 and part of 61) is very complicated and forms a pronounced salient. In the evening	A R [illegible]

Original
10

Instructions regarding War Diaries and Intelligence Summaries are contained in F. S. Regs., Part II. and the Staff Manual respectively. Title pages will be prepared in manuscript.

WAR DIARY
or
INTELLIGENCE SUMMARY.
(*Erase heading not required.*)

Army Form C. 2118.

Hour, Date, Place	Summary of Events and Information	Remarks and references to Appendices
June 28th continued	D Coy less 1 platoon relieved Gloster Coy in 63 trench. Following were new dispositions. A Coy sent ½ platoon B Coy 1 platoon to [illegible] behind 62, 61 trenches. C Coy 1 platoon to support trenches on left near RUE DE BOIS village and D Coy 1 platoon to support trenches on right of [illegible]. Dug out now [illegible] in 2nd support line - built by the Welsh Fusiliers. A quiet day	
June 29th trenches	A quiet day. Showery and colder. The dug out at Headquarters not at all comfortable. [illegible] is the order of the day! C.O. went on leave in the morning.	
June 30th trenches to billets	G.O.C. 81st Bde and new Bde Major Captain Tidswell D.S.O. The Leicestershire Regt. New communication trenches sited and begun. In evening A, B and D coys were relieved and marched back to billets. C Coy to G H Q line. Relief [illegible].	

A R B[illegible]
Capt

(73989) W4141—463. 400,000. 9/14. H.&J.Ltd. Forms/C. 2118/10.

addenda original

Instructions regarding War Diaries and Intelligence Summaries are contained in F. S. Regs., Part II. and the Staff Manual respectively. Title pages will be prepared in manuscript.

WAR DIARY
or
INTELLIGENCE SUMMARY.
(*Erase heading not required.*)

Army Form C. 2118.

Hour, Date, Place	Summary of Events and Information	Remarks and references to Appendices
During the month of June, the following honours and distinctions were given to Officers N.C.O. and men in the 1/A&SH.		
Mentioned in despatches	Lt Col H.B. Kerr Captains Porteous D.S.O, Boyle, Pullar, Young, Lt Gibb [illegible] [illegible] McAlister, Pte Gray, Cleary and L/Cpl Grant	
	C.S.M. Robb, L/Cpl Sinclair, Sergt Yearsley, Pte Coombe, Pte Lamb	
D.C.M.		
Military Cross	Captain & Adjt A.R. Boyle, Capt J.H. Young	
	2/Lt J. Neill. "For conspicuous good work since Dec 19th 1914 and especially on May 11th 1915 near Hooge when his coolness and skill in leading his men were most marked. He also showed great gallantry in leading a counter attack in the course of which he was severely wounded. He collected and took forward about 100 men who were falling back in some disorder at a very critical moment."	
Red ticket from G.O.C. 27th Div	2/Lt J Bollin	
Green tickets do do. do.	Captain W.G. Neilson, Lt J. O'Driscoll RAMC MO i/c 2/Lt R Gibb C.S.M. Plummer (5274) Sgt Eadie (7718) Sgt Kerr (10384) Sgt Smellie (9830) Sgt Yearsley (10277) Corporal Simpson (257) L/Cpl Hood (2644) L/Cpl Paul (9215) L/Cpl Wilson (6097) Ptes Darling (213) Davis (5481) Kerr (4067) Lynch (556) McMillan (53) McInnes (1857) Service (151) Stewart (10714) Tibbs (7139)	

A.R. Boyle Capt

(73989) W4141—463. 400,000. 9/14. H.&J.Ltd. Forms/C. 2118/10.

War Diary

June 1–30

[illegible]
Capt
Adjt [illegible]

V 6

81st Inf.Bde.
27th Div.

WAR DIARY

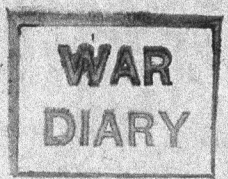

1st BATTN. THE ARGYLL & SUTHERLAND HIGHLANDERS.

J U L Y

1 9 1 5

V 6

81st Inf.Bde.
27th Div.

WAR DIARY

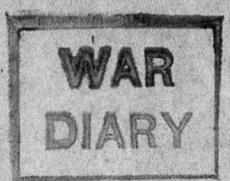

1st BATTN. THE ARGYLL & SUTHERLAND HIGHLANDERS.

J U L Y

1 9 1 5

1. Original

Instructions regarding War Diaries and Intelligence Summaries are contained in F. S. Regs., Part II. and the Staff Manual respectively. Title pages will be prepared in manuscript.

WAR DIARY
or
~~INTELLIGENCE SUMMARY.~~
(*Erase heading not required.*)

Army Form C. 2118.

Hour, Date, Place	Summary of Events and Information	Remarks and references to Appendices
July 1st Billets	A quiet day in billets - nothing to report. 1st class from Brigade bomb school returned	
July 2nd Billets	Routine. Nothing of any interest to report. 2nd class went to bomb school	
July 3rd Billets	Baths for A & D Coys, M.G. and HQrs in the morning. D Coy relieved C Coy in G.H.Q. line in the evening. The usual quiet day with Coys under their officers	
July 4th Billets	Church parade in one billets in morning - beyond this nothing but routine work.	
July 5th Billets	Routine - nothing to report	
July 6th Billets to trenches	Baths for unwashed men at 10.45 a.m. and 3.45 p.m. Relief in the evening. Much practice in the Glorious and [illegible] in making repairs in all trenches much quicker and better carried out	
July 7th Trenches	The usual trench day - much work planned and begun. C.O. went tour of trenches in the afternoon	
July 8th Trenches	Work on communication trenches progressing well. It is proposed to have a communication trench	A.R. Boyle Capt. 1/A&S.H.

(73989) W4141—463. 400,000. 9/14. H.&J.Ltd. Forms/C. 2118/10.

2. Original

Instructions regarding War Diaries and Intelligence Summaries are contained in F. S. Regs., Part II. and the Staff Manual respectively. Title pages will be prepared in manuscript.

WAR DIARY
or
~~INTELLIGENCE SUMMARY.~~
(*Erase heading not required.*)

Army Form C. 2118.

Hour, Date, Place	Summary of Events and Information	Remarks and references to Appendices
July 8th Continued	every fifty yards from support trench to firing line. A long trench from Hqrs line to support line was also begun and good progress made. D Coy doing good work. A very quiet peaceful existence with few shells or bullets and all ranks very happy	
July 9th trenches	The usual work during the day. In the evening interest was added by a message from the Brigade warning us to be extra vigilant as the enemy were expected to show increased activity. Large bodies of Germans had been seen near PERENCHIES. The night, however, passed as quietly as usual and our patrols reported our own wire to be in a good condition and no enemy's patrols out	
July 10th trenches	The usual trench day. Major Singer commanding 17th Coy R E went round trenches in the evening with the C.O. A new rifle battery was sited and constructed to fire into WEZ MACQUART. Two men wounded whilst patrolling in the evening, the enemy showing rather more activity than usual. Patrols report enemy's wire strong and being daily strengthened	

a R Boyle Capt
1/R.O.S.H.

(73989) W4141—463. 400,000. 9/14. H.&J.Ltd. Forms/C. 2118/10.

original

3.

Instructions regarding War Diaries and Intelligence Summaries are contained in F. S. Regs., Part II. and the Staff Manual respectively. Title pages will be prepared in manuscript.

WAR DIARY
or
~~INTELLIGENCE~~ SUMMARY.
(Erase heading not required.)

Army Form C. 2118.

Hour, Date, Place	Summary of Events and Information	Remarks and references to Appendices
July 11th trenches	C O discussed best method of strengthening wire entanglements by putting in iron posts amongst the wooden ones – about 100 of the former being issued at night. The usual trench work day and night.	
July 12th trenches to billets	Relieved in evening by Gloster Regt. and marched back to same billet in ARMENTIÈRES. The last tour in the trenches has been very ~~[illegible]~~ pleasant – weather good much work done and trenches much improved and strengthened.	
July 13th billets	A normal day in billets. Men granted passes 30% per coy.	
July 14th billets	French national fête day – shells were expected and duly arrived. A showery day. The cellars had been inspected overnight – and on the first shell arriving in the garden at the back of men's billets all men were sent to the cellars. The quarter master's store had several shells all round it, and the officers Mess billet had one into the garden and two in the street outside, the second of these wounding the mess cart driver (Bowgunfor) since died of wounds, Lance Corpl a signaller and Capt. Cooper. All windows broken and one bicycle destroyed.	A R Boyle Capt 1/Dorset R

4 original

Instructions regarding War Diaries and Intelligence Summaries are contained in F. S. Regs., Part II. and the Staff Manual respectively. Title pages will be prepared in manuscript.

WAR DIARY
or
~~INTELLIGENCE SUMMARY~~.

(Erase heading not required.)

Army Form C. 2118.

Hour, Date, Place	Summary of Events and Information	Remarks and references to Appendices
July 15th billets	Smoke helmets of B. C and D Coys sprayed with special solution to keep them damp and efficient. Otherwise nothing out of the ordinary to report. B Coy relieved A in trenches on G.H.Q. line now called BOIS GRENIER line	
July 16th billets	Pte McGregor buried in Erquinghem 3 p.m. Working party in the evening. Otherwise nothing to report.	
July 17th billets	~~Smoke helmets~~ of A Coy and details sprayed. In the afternoon companies moved from billets to billets vacated by 4th R.B. 80th Bde — All accomodated in large factories or workshops attached. Most of the buildings in Armentières are factories for making of cloth etc. Sanitary arrangements in billets bad. HQrs in a large bourgeois house with very pronounced nouveau art fittings?, moving there in the evening. B Coy returned from BOIS GRENIER line about midnight relieved by 1 Coy of Glosters on the line being shortened. The 50th Division now on our left having Armentières as billeting area and the trenches N. of Chapelle d'Armentières — Lille Road. 81st Bde have them from this road to railway RUE du BOIS	A R Boyle Capt 1/8/16

5 original

Instructions regarding War Diaries and Intelligence Summaries are contained in F. S. Regs., Part II. and the Staff Manual respectively. Title pages will be prepared in manuscript.

WAR DIARY
or
~~INTELLIGENCE~~ SUMMARY.

(*Erase heading not required.*)

Army Form C. 2118.

Hour, Date, Place	Summary of Events and Information	Remarks and references to Appendices
July 18th billets to trenches	Church for all persuasions in the morning. Captain B. J. Lang came to see us from L. of C. In the evening relieved trenches held by Glosters Nos 60, 61, 62 being taken over by D, B and C respectively. A Coy to BOIS GRENIER line. Gloster Regt very pleased with amount of work battalion had done last time in trenches.	
July 19th trenches	Work on a new communication trench from Bn Hqrs back to Chapelle d'Armentières road begun. All men doing field punishment being employed all day. Capt Lang visited trenches.	
July 20th trenches	G.O.C. 81st I. B. went round trenches, and visited 59 trench now held by R. I. Fusiliers 82nd Bde to be taken over by A Coy in the evening. Our artillery very active, ammunition shortage seemingly having finished! A Coy took over 59 trench in the evening	
July 21st trenches	Pte. McAteer court-martialled at Hqrs. in the morning for sleeping on his post. Cameron [illegible] in [illegible] of A Coy who had done excellent work. Pte. Hay [illegible] and reconnoitring since beginning of June, [illegible] reported missing. He and two others were lying out on patrol near German wire. Time came to return [illegible]	A. R. Boyle Capt 1/R.S.F.[?]

(73989) W4141—463. 400,000. 9/14. H.&J.Ltd. Forms/C. 2118/10.

6 original

Instructions regarding War Diaries and Intelligence Summaries are contained in F. S. Regs., Part II. and the Staff Manual respectively. Title pages will be prepared in manuscript.

WAR DIARY
or
~~INTELLIGENCE~~ SUMMARY.
(*Erase heading not required.*)

Army Form C. 2118.

Hour, Date, Place	Summary of Events and Information	Remarks and references to Appendices
July 21st - continued	our trenches and Maybank ordered the two with him to crawl back while he covered their retreat. Soon after they had gone, he sighted a German patrol to his front and against orders emptied his magazine into them. This firing brought out another patrol who got between Maybank and the other two who at once fired on this second patrol with good results. ~~They~~ These two men eventually regained our trench soon after dawn but Maybank did not return. In the evening the enemy opposite 60 sent over some rifle grenades wounding a few men. We replied with some well directed ones, which produced shouts and groans but the Germans had the last say ~~[illegible]~~ just before the ration party went off, and we did not answer because of the ration parties - postponing our reply till the following day. A patrol go[ne] out to look for Maybank or his body could find no traces.	
July 22nd trenches	The reply to the German rifle grenades of ~~[illegible]~~ last night began at 3.00 a.m. B and C and D Coys were ordered to fire 15 rifle grenades each at enemy's trenches and the large and small trench mortars were ordered to fire 10 rounds apiece. This was done, a breach made in	A R Boyle Capt 1/4 A&S H

7 original

Instructions regarding War Diaries and Intelligence Summaries are contained in F. S. Regs., Part II. and the Staff Manual respectively. Title pages will be prepared in manuscript.

WAR DIARY
or
~~INTELLIGENCE SUMMARY.~~

(Erase heading not required.)

Army Form C. 2118.

Hour, Date, Place	Summary of Events and Information	Remarks and references to Appendices
July 22nd continued	enemy's parapet, and a machine played on to this gap. It was quite a successful "hate" and only produced a few whizz bangs and and 12 rifle grenades in answer. The day passed quietly, work proceeding well.	
July 23rd trenches	Sergeant Robertson D Coy lately returned from the M. Gun shot through the head whilst foolishly keeping his head above the parapet. Otherwise a normal day	
July 24th trenches	Lt. Col. Dave and Major Nisbet of Glosters visited 59 [illegible] in the morning. A showery day – work as usual.	
July 25th trenches to billets	A few well grouped but innocuous field gun shells fell behind Hqrs. in the afternoon – otherwise a quiet day. Relieved in the evening by Glosters. C Coy going to BOIS GRENIER [illegible]. Much excellent work had been done during the tour – second line made fire [illegible]. Field of fire improved its artillery [illegible] behind all breast works, communication trenches boarded [illegible].	

C.R. Boyle Capt
1/Bucks Bn

8 original

Instructions regarding War Diaries and Intelligence Summaries are contained in F. S. Regs., Part II. and the Staff Manual respectively. Title pages will be prepared in manuscript.

WAR DIARY
or
~~INTELLIGENCE~~ SUMMARY.
(Erase heading not required.)

Army Form C. 2118.

Hour, Date, Place	Summary of Events and Information	Remarks and references to Appendices
July 26th billets	The usual cleaning up work for first day in billets with nothing to report.	
July 27th billets	Brigade Armourer began inspection of rifles. Smoke helmets sprayed. G.O.C. 8th Bde visited Bn Hqrs. A working party of 200 in the evening started on breast-work communication trenches for winter use!	
July 28th billets	Lt Mackay proceeded on leave. Usual routine. The men's billets very uncomfortable and drunkenness rather prevalent.	
July 29th billets	D Coy commanded by Lt Greenfield relieved C Coy in BOIS GRENIER line in the evening. Nothing of any interest to report.	
July 30th billets	Lt G. I. Campbell returned from leave and took over command of D Coy. Ordinary routine.	
July 31st billets	In the evening the divisional artillery opened on German trenches and wire opposite RUE de BOIS. In view of possible reprisals all men were ordered to be in billets by 6 p.m. But only two shells were sent near the billets and men who [illegible] headquarters' cellars soon emerged. Word received that 2nd [illegible] Territorial [illegible] had landed at Boulogne.	A R Boyle Capt [illegible]

(73989) W4141—463. 400,000. 9/14. H.&J.Ltd. Forms/C. 2118/10.

N7

81st Inf.Bde.
27th Div.

WAR
DIARY

1st BATTN. THE ARGYLL & SUTHERLAND HIGHLANDERS.

A U G U S T

1 9 1 5

Original 1

Instructions regarding War Diaries and Intelligence Summaries are contained in F. S. Regs., Part II. and the Staff Manual respectively. Title pages will be prepared in manuscript.

WAR DIARY
or
~~INTELLIGENCE SUMMARY.~~

(Erase heading not required.)

August

Army Form C. 2118.

1/A&SHdrs.

Hour, Date, Place	Summary of Events and Information	Remarks and references to Appendices
Aug 1st 1915 ARMENTIERES	Lt Col H L Henderson arrived on return from sick leave about 5 a.m. Orders re move to rest area received. Church parade in morning	
Aug 2nd 1915 " to JESUS FARM	Battalion marched to new billets by companies starting about 2 p.m. D Coy were relieved in BOIS GRENIER line by a company 4th R.B. and marched back by night. Major Elphinstone assumed command of D Coy. Battalion billets in vicinity of JESUS FARM B 26 D BELGIUM sheet 36.	
Aug 3rd JESUS FARM	A rainy day. Companies at work settling down, improving billets and shelters, sanitary arrangements etc.	
Aug 4th "	Companies under Coy. officers drilling, physical exercises, fire control etc. This the first opportunity for any form of continuous training since arrival in the country. Men very happy – plenty of football etc. G.O.C. 81st I.B. visited Bn Hqrs in afternoon.	
Aug 5th "	Company work continued. Lt Col Henderson to 81st I. Bde Hqrs ERQUINGHEM in the morning to take over command of 81st I. Bde, G.O.C. having gone on leave	C R Boyle capt adjt 1/A&SH

Original 2

Instructions regarding War Diaries and Intelligence Summaries are contained in F. S. Regs., Part II. and the Staff Manual respectively. Title pages will be prepared in manuscript.

WAR DIARY
or
~~INTELLIGENCE SUMMARY.~~
(*Erase heading not required.*)

Army Form C. 2118.

Hour, Date, Place	Summary of Events and Information	Remarks and references to Appendices
Aug 6th JESUS FARM	Ordinary routine and company work in the morning and play in the afternoon. A football league started.	3 strength 7th Aug. 26 Officers ? 986 O.R. ?
Aug 7th " "	Work as usual in morning and in afternoon the Regimental team played Camerons at football but were beaten by 1–0. Men played in the field.	
Aug 8th " "	Church parades for all denominations in the morning at various places. C of S at Hqrs Farm.	
Aug 9th " "	A digging scheme on a defended post at BOIS GRENIER begun under the superintendence of Capt. Wilson. A permanent party of 50 men and 1 officer by day and 200 men and 4 officers by night. Lts Gunn, Gillespie and McAlister detailed to assist Capt Wilson one of them being always engaged on the work. Lt Rodger O C Grenadier Coy. began class for instruction of men [illegible] to be trained as bomb throwers and all subalterns.	
Aug 10th " "	G O C 1st Army with Maj Gen Butler (late Lancashire Fusiliers) visited billets in evening. Normal work during the day.	A R Boyle Capt. Adjt 1/ [illegible]

(73989) W4141—463. 400,000. 9/14. H.&J.Ltd. Forms/C. 2118/10.

Original 3

WAR DIARY
or
~~INTELLIGENCE SUMMARY.~~
(*Erase heading not required.*)

Army Form C. 2118.

Instructions regarding War Diaries and Intelligence Summaries are contained in F. S. Regs., Part II. and the Staff Manual respectively. Title pages will be prepared in manuscript.

Hour, Date, Place	Summary of Events and Information	Remarks and references to Appendices
Aug 11th JESUS FARM	Adjutant to Brigade Hqrs to hear details of new trenches to be taken over from 82nd Bde. Work as usual. Bathing takes places every day in the canal.	
Aug 12th "	Adjutant visited new trenches – 50, 51, 52, 53 in front BOIS GRENIER. Trenches held by 2/Leinster Regt in I 31 B, I 32 A. sheet 36 Belgium. Trenches good but communication trenches scarce. Arranged details with adjt Leinsters	
Aug 13th "	C.O. returned from Hqrs 81st I. Bde. Companies went to hot baths in ERQUINGHEM. Company grenadier company, M.G. and Hqrs representatives visited trenches in morning. Captain A.W.R. Sprot now adjutant of 8th Entrenching Batt. bivouacked near B 2 D sheet 36 Belgium – visited battalion	
Aug 14th "	Maj. Elphinstone returned from leave. 8th Division horse show near SAILLY. 2nd Batt. in billets in LAVENTIE	A R Boyle capt adjt 1/A&SH
	Strength. 26 officers } 978 O.R }	

(73989) W4141—463. 400,000. 9/14. H.&J.Ltd. Forms/C. 2118/10.

Original 4

Instructions regarding War Diaries and Intelligence Summaries are contained in F. S. Regs., Part II. and the Staff Manual respectively. Title pages will be prepared in manuscript.

WAR DIARY
or
~~INTELLIGENCE SUMMARY.~~
(Erase heading not required.)

Army Form C. 2118.

Hour, Date, Place	Summary of Events and Information	Remarks and references to Appendices
Aug 15th JESUS FARM	C.O and adjt went to visit trenches 50–53 meeting G.O.C 81st I. Bde. in BOIS GRENIER. Trenches very wet and weather making progress difficult. Church parades cancelled owing to weather but celebration of Holy communion by Rev. A. Gilchrist was possible in the evening. Work on BOIS GRENIER defence stopped.	
Aug 16th JESUS FARM to trenches	Last day of rest – the best rest battalion has had since arrival in France. Much useful work (drill handling of arms, physical drill, musketry) has been done – men looking much smarter and very well equipped. Numbers of men reporting sick rather above the average as there have been many foot-ball knees etc. The officers played the Cameron officers at football during this rest – the match being drawn 1 goal each. Football league won by A Coy who beat transport and grooms in the final. A cross country race won by D Coy – but spoilt because A Coy team took the wrong course. Bathing and fishing much appreciated. The local farmers were helped by some of the men with the harvest.	
	At 10.30 a.m. General Sir W. Pulteney – G.O.C 3rd Corps inspected the battalion which was drawn up in mass facing East. G.O.C 27th Divn and 81st I. Bde accompanied him. Sir W. Pulteney.	A R Boyle Capt adjt 1/A&SH

Original 5

Instructions regarding War Diaries and Intelligence Summaries are contained in F. S. Regs., Part II. and the Staff Manual respectively. Title pages will be prepared in manuscript.

WAR DIARY
or
~~INTELLIGENCE SUMMARY.~~
(*Erase heading not required.*)

Army Form C. 2118.

Hour, Date, Place	Summary of Events and Information	Remarks and references to Appendices
Aug 16th continued	inspected every company, the Grenadier coy, M.G. Signallers and stretcher bearers very closely and expressed himself as very pleased indeed at such a fine turn out and the look of the men. Other staff officers equally complimentary. In the evening companies marched at 15 minutes interval to relieve [illegible] Regt in trenches 50-53 A Coy leading and taking over 50 trench; the remainder in alphabetical order from the right (50). A heavy thunderstorm had made trenches very muddy and slippery but relief was fairly quick and well carried out. Two platoons - 1 from B and 1 from D in support line - also bombers etc in support line near store. The grenadier company will probably take a large part in future operations. 1 coy. of Gloster Regt in reserve in BOIS GRENIER line. A quiet night.	
Aug 17th trenches	A thundery showery day, trenches very dirty indeed and much work was required to drain them. It was very difficult carrying water along 1200 yards and more of SHAFTESBURY AVENUE the main communication trench from BOIS GRENIER. C.O. and adjt. sent for to [illegible] I. Bde Hqrs to hear details of lengthening of line at present held by the Brigade - two more trenches having to be taken over.	A R B[illegible] Capt adjt 1/[illegible]

Original 6

Instructions regarding War Diaries and Intelligence Summaries are contained in F. S. Regs., Part II. and the Staff Manual respectively. Title pages will be prepared in manuscript.

WAR DIARY
or
~~INTELLIGENCE SUMMARY.~~

(*Erase heading not required.*)

Army Form C. 2118.

Hour, Date, Place	Summary of Events and Information	Remarks and references to Appendices
Aug 18th Trenches	A normal trench day. In the evening A Coy was relieved by 1 Coy of Gloster Regt. and marched back to billets in RUE DELETTREE H 23 A sheet 36 Belgium. Lateral defences of SHAFTESBURY AVENUE taken in hand and loopholes removed, firing parapet being everywhere substituted. A quiet night.	
Aug 19th Trenches	Pte Mallam D Coy shot through the head and buried in BOIS GRENIER. Work as usual – much to be done.	
Aug 20th Trenches	C.O went round trenches in the morning. Major Sutton Wessex Fd. Coy R E promised much help with boards, pumps, water tanks etc. Good patrol work by B Coy at night discovered working party on enemy's wire with covering party in front, which was fired at by M Guns	
Aug 21st Trenches	G.O.C 81st I. Bde to Battalion Hqrs in the morning. Three dead Germans the products of the M.G. "strafe" over-night were seen on the parapet. A wet day.	
	Strength 25 officers } 962 O.R. }	A R Boyle Capt Adjt 1/A&SH.

(73989) W4141—463. 400,000. 9/14. H.&J.Ltd. Forms/C. 2118/10.

Original 7

Instructions regarding War Diaries and Intelligence Summaries are contained in F. S. Regs., Part II. and the Staff Manual respectively. Title pages will be prepared in manuscript.

WAR DIARY
or
~~INTELLIGENCE SUMMARY.~~
(*Erase heading not required.*)

Army Form C. 2118.

Hour, Date, Place		Summary of Events and Information	Remarks and references to Appendices
Aug. 22nd	Trenches	A telegram came in the morning announcing that leave and packet of boats had been stopped. Aeroplanes very active, one of ours brought down opposite 51 trench. Lt TAYLOR rejoined battalion from 8th Entrenching Battn – posted to B Coy.	
Aug 23rd	"	A normal day. G.O.C went round trenches in morning. Enemy working party reported in evening and fired on.	
Aug 24th	"	A normal trench day – work as usual. Nothing special to report	
Aug 25th	"	Work as usual – a hot fine day.	
Aug 26th	"	C.O and 2nd in command visited Gloster Hqrs to learn details of 48 and 49 trenches which are to be taken over on Sept 6th. Nothing to report.	ARBorle Capt Adjt 1/Argylls
Aug 27th	"	Adjt visited Gloster Hqrs. A normal day. Bde. general Romer 3rd Corps and Lt Col. Cory G.S.O1 27th Divn visited trenches. Many assembly trenches being dug behind.	

Original 8

Instructions regarding War Diaries and Intelligence Summaries are contained in F. S. Regs., Part II. and the Staff Manual respectively. Title pages will be prepared in manuscript.

WAR DIARY

~~or~~

~~INTELLIGENCE SUMMARY~~.

(*Erase heading not required.*)

Army Form C. 2118.

Hour, Date, Place		Summary of Events and Information	Remarks and references to Appendices
Aug. 28th	Trenches	G.O.C 27th Division visited trenches. A showery day with nothing out of the ordinary to report.	Strength 28th Aug. 26 officers, 972 O.R.
Aug 29th	"	Adjutant went on leave. G.O.C 81st I.B. visited trenches. Rain came on in afternoon and continued through night.	
Aug 30th	trenches to billets	The battalion was relieved in trenches by 2nd Camerons and marched to billets RUE DELETTREÉE H.23A sheet 36 Belgium. Relief very quick.	
Aug 31st	Billets RUE DELETTREÉE	Captain Wilson went on leave also Captain O'Driscoll R.A.M.C. Routine work during the day.	

A R Boyle Capt
adjt 1/A&SH

V 8

81st Inf.Bde.
27th Div.

WAR DIARY

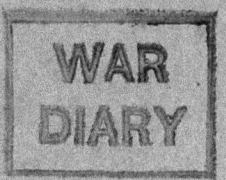

1st BATTN. THE ARGYLL & SUTHERLAND HIGHLANDERS.

S E P T E M B E R

1 9 1 5

121

Instructions regarding War Diaries and Intelligence Summaries are contained in F. S. Regs., Part II. and the Staff Manual respectively. Title pages will be prepared in manuscript.

WAR DIARY
or
~~INTELLIGENCE~~ SUMMARY.
(*Erase heading not required.*)

Army Form C. 2118.

Hour, Date, Place		Summary of Events and Information	Remarks and references to Appendices
Sept 1st	RUE DE L'EPINETTE REEL H23A sheet 36	A wet day. Battalion provided digging party at night. Lt. McCutcheon went on leave	
Sept 2nd	"	Routine work. Digging party by day. Strength 26 officers 971 O.R.	
Sept 3rd	"	A cold wet [illegible] which prevented digging party from going out.	
Sept 4th	"	Second Lt. Clark late corporal [illegible] and 2nd Lt Smiley late Corpl 1st Royal Dragoons, joined and posted to B and C Coys respectively. Lt. Rodger proceeded to join Hqrs. Divisional R.E. 27th Divn after excellent work as Grenade officer.	
Sept 5th	"	Church parade in morning interrupted by rain. 320 men digging in the evening.	
Sept 6th	Billets to trenches BOIS GRENIER	Adjutant returned from leave, and instructions then came to be taken over from Cameronians. In evening marched to relieve Cameronians. A Coy to 50, B to 51, C to 52, D 53 trench. Major Elphinstone to rest station [illegible] with poisoned foot.	

(73989) W4141—463. 400,000. 9/14. H.&J.Ltd. Forms/C. 2118/10.

Instructions regarding War Diaries and Intelligence Summaries are contained in F. S. Regs., Part II. and the Staff Manual respectively. Title pages will be prepared in manuscript.

INTELLIGENCE SUMMARY

(Erase heading not required.)

Hour, Date, Place	Summary of Events and Information	Remarks and references to Appendices
Sept 7th Trenches	Work in trenches continued, also artillery registration which made much noise and produced occasional reprisals. Captain Sprot came to trenches to visit Hqrs. Nothing else of interest.	
Sept 8th "	A quieter day with usual routine work.	
Sept 9th "	C.O. and adjutant to 8th I. Bde in afternoon to hear plans for the future operations and likely developments given as secret. Normal routine. 28 officers 993 O.R.	
Sept 10th "	Hqrs and 2 Coys 11th W. Yorkshire Regt. attached for instruction. Enemy very jumpy in the evening.	
Sept 11th "	Machine guns and 2 coys 11th W. Yorks relieved Coys and Hqrs of same battalion already in trenches. Two platoons of each coy attached to a company of 1/A.&S.H. Corporal [illegible] with pair of Bagpipes rejoined Battalion after [illegible]. Very welcome.	
Sept 12th "	Our field guns shelled Rue du Bois enemy trenches with new explosive – enemy retaliating on our trenches and ground in rear of Rue du Bois. Attached W. Yorks coys etc. returned to billets.	C.R. [illegible] Capt 1/A.&S.H.

1247 W 3299 200,000 (E) 8/14 J.B.C. & A. Forms/C. 2118/11.

Instructions regarding War Diaries and Intelligence Summaries are contained in F. S. Regs., Part II. and the Staff Manual respectively. Title pages will be prepared in manuscript.

3.

~~WAR DIARY~~ or INTELLIGENCE SUMMARY

(Erase heading not required.)

Hour, Date, Place	Summary of Events and Information	Remarks and references to Appendices
Sept 13th trenches BOIS GRENIER	German aeroplane descended near STEENWERCK and occupants gallantly opened fire on a company of 80th Bde hoping to [illegible] engine [illegible] - the company returned fire and killed both pilot and observer - machine badly damaged. At about 5.30 a.m. a mine was exploded under or near parapet of one of 8th Divn trenches and crater [illegible] violently shelled - but our artillery soon opened on enemy's trenches and stopped their artillery. A day of artillery activity - field guns again testing H.E. against [illegible] - Heavies opposite 56, 57 and field guns opposite 50 and 51 firing with good effect. 2 in morning [illegible] trench mortar registering on [illegible] sap brought a reply of several [illegible] bombs which killed 2 men and wounded 4. Hqrs and 2 coys 10th West Riding Regt attached for instruction and distributed as before.	
Sept 14th "	Guns of a new division registered on enemy trenches - several [illegible] [illegible]. Other [illegible] were coming in all day. Two coys and machine guns 10th W Riding relieved above 2 coys in trenches.	W.R.B[illegible] Capt [illegible]

1247 W 3299 200,000 (E) 8/14 J.B.C. & A. Forms/C. 2118/11.

Instructions regarding War Diaries and Intelligence Summaries are contained in F. S. Regs., Part II. and the Staff Manual respectively. Title pages will be prepared in manuscript.

4.

INTELLIGENCE SUMMARY

(Erase heading not required.)

Hour, Date, Place	Summary of Events and Information	Remarks and references to Appendices
Sept 15th trenches to JESUS FARM	Lt. Thorneycroft sent on at 9 a.m. to billet battalion in new area. Relief in evening. 50 and 51 trenches taken over by 1st R. I. Rifles. 52 and 53 by coy of 10th [illegible] Battn. & all present attached [illegible] from [illegible]. Quick relief.	
Sept 16th JESUS FARM	Battalion spent day getting clean – same billets as before. Hqrs in a different farm. [illegible] Capt Sprott came to tea.	
Sept 17th JESUS FARM to BLEU	Marched from JESUS FARM to BLEU a small pretty village near VIEUX BERQUIN to N.W. of HAZEBROUCK sheet 5A. Fair billets – hot day but few men fell out	
Sept 18th BLEU	G.O.C. 3rd corps (Sir W. Pulteney) inspected 3rd I.B. about 1 mile from BLEU wishing Brigade goodbye and thanking them for good work in trenches at ARMENTIERES. A fine, hot day	
Sept 19th BLEU to HAZEBROUCK	Church parade in morning. Marched in the evening to HAZEBROUCK Rly station. Paraded 8 pm arrived 11 pm – entrained by midnight very quickly	[illegible] Capt [illegible]

1247 W 3299 200,000 (E) 8/14 J.B.C. & A. Forms/C. 2118/11.

Instructions regarding War Diaries and Intelligence Summaries are contained in F. S. Regs., Part II. and the Staff Manual respectively. Title pages will be prepared in manuscript.

5

~~WAR DIARY~~ or INTELLIGENCE SUMMARY

(Erase heading not required.)

Hour, Date, Place		Summary of Events and Information	Remarks and references to Appendices
Sept 20th	HAZEBROUCK to LAMOTTE EN SANTERRE AMIENS sheet 12	Arrived GUILLAUCOURT (ref MONTDIDIER sheet 21) at 11 a.m. – very quick detrainment – rested and had a meal in a field near station. Marched to LAMOTTE EN SANTERRE where billeting party of 5 N.C.O.s had arranged bivouacs and billets – the latter very scarce owing to large number of troops and staff of Division and Brigade being in the village.	
Sept 21st	LAMOTTE en SANTERRE	Settling down – nothing to report.	
Sept 22nd	"	Orders issued re inspection of battalion by 3rd Army Commander cancelled soon afterwards. Coys under Coy commanders. Transport moved to CAILLY.	
Sept 23rd	"	The Battalion was inspected by G.O.C 3rd Army who was accompanied by G.O.C 12th Corps, 27th Divn, 80th Bde. Battalion paraded in mass on left of Camerons. G.O.C expressed himself as very pleased at turn out and general appearance of the men who were very clean considering short notice they were given to prepare, in no case more than 2 hours. Drew marching order without packs. In this connection the following was sent to 27th Divn from 12th Corps – and forwarded for information of the battalion. Begins	[illegible] Capt Adjt

1247 W 3299 200,000 (E) 8/14 J.B.C. & A. Forms/C. 2118/11.

Instructions regarding War Diaries and Intelligence Summaries are contained in F. S. Regs., Part II. and the Staff Manual respectively. Title pages will be prepared in manuscript.

6

INTELLIGENCE SUMMARY

(Erase heading not required.)

Hour, Date, Place	Summary of Events and Information	Remarks and references to Appendices
Sept 23rd continued	"The corps commander wishes to convey his own and the Army Commanders satisfaction at the fine appearance presented by the 2nd Battn Cameron Hdrs and 1st Battn Argyll & Sutherland Highlanders on parade on the 23rd and the smart soldierlike bearing of these battalions and the manner in which they handled their arms reflect great credit on the G.O.C. 27th Divn and the Brigade and Battalion commanders concerned. Will you kindly make known to all ranks of these battalions how pleased the Army and the Corps commanders were at what they saw of them on the 23rd – Signed Staff Major for Bde. Genl Strength 28 officers 983 O.R.	
Sept 24th billets	– Companies under O.C. Coys – ordinary routine work.	
Sept 25th "	A showery day. Good news of French & British advance in the evening – ordinary routine work during day. [illegible] moved to PROYART.	
Sept 26th "	– R.C. and C of E church parade in morning and Coy route marching in afternoon. Battn. Hqrs moved to house billets occupied by 3rd [illegible] Hqrs on their removal to PROYART. A big comfortable house.	
		[illegible] Capt [illegible]

1247 W 3299 200,000 (E) 8/14 J.B.C. & A. Forms/C. 2118/11.

Instructions regarding War Diaries and Intelligence Summaries are contained in F. S. Regs., Part II. and the Staff Manual respectively. Title pages will be prepared in manuscript.

~~WAR DIARY~~ or **INTELLIGENCE SUMMARY.**
(Erase heading not required.)

Hour, Date, Place	Summary of Events and Information	Remarks and references to Appendices
Sept 27th billets LAMOTTE EN SANTERRE	Companies under O.C. Coys. after a battalion parade on which the C.O addressed the troops re C in C's message which stated that he was convinced that every officer N.C.O and man would exert himself to the utmost.	
Sept 28th billets	Bt. Lt Col H.B. Kidd received intimation that he had been given command of a Brigade. After saying goodbye to G.O.C. 81st I.B. he left in evening by train from MARCELCAVE to report at War Office. Companies practised open fighting etc	
Sept 29th billets	Company work. Smoke helmets sprayed in the afternoon. 2000 sandbags drawn from FROISSY and 3 issued to all ranks to carry with their equipment.	
Sept 30th billets	A normal day. Company work as usual.	[illegible]

(73989) W4141—463. 400,000. 9/14. H.&J.Ltd. Forms/C. 2118/10.

V9

81st Inf.Bde.
27th Div.

WAR
DIARY

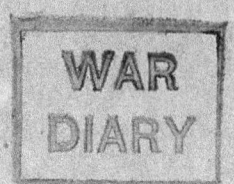

1st BATTN. THE ARGYLL & SUTHERLAND HIGHLANDERS.

O C T O B E R

1 9 1 5

A.G.'s Office
3rd Echelon
Base

Memo:

Herewith war diary 1st Bn A & S H. for period 1st – 31st Oct.
Please acknowledge receipt

10.XI.15

A R Boyle Capt.
1st Bn Argyll & Sutherland Highlanders

Instructions regarding War Diaries and Intelligence Summaries are contained in F. S. Regs., Part II. and the Staff Manual respectively. Title pages will be prepared in manuscript.

Original

WAR DIARY
or
~~INTELLIGENCE SUMMARY.~~
(*Erase heading not required.*)

Army Form C. 2118.

Hour, Date, Place	Summary of Events and Information	Remarks and references to Appendices
Oct 1st Billets LAMOTTE en SANTERRE Map: sheet 12 AMIENS	Two companies marched to MÉRICOURT to have kilts disinfected which process destroyed the lice but also the shape of the kilt. Otherwise a normal day - companies working under company officers. In the afternoon the 12th Battalion (Lt. Col. C. Davidson) marched from VILLERS BRETONNEUX to visit us - the men had tea in a field near the village and the officers were divided among companies. Several old 1st Batt. N.C.O. & men were seen, including Pipe Major Douglas. A very fine lot of men, and well turned out.	
Oct 2nd - billets	A normal day. The 12th Batt. passed through the village on its way to the trenches for instruction. Kilt disinfection continued.	Strength 24 officers 939 O.R.
Oct 3rd billets	Church parade for all denominations. Billeting parties marched to CHUIGNOLLES in the afternoon to see dispositions of Leinster Regt now in that place. A Leinster billeting party equally came to LAMOTTE. Orders re move to trenches issued.	
Oct 4th LAMOTTE to CHUIGNOLLES	The battalion marched to CHUIGNOLLES via MÉRICOURT arriving at former place at 11.30 a.m. and taking over billets from 1st Bn. Leinster Regt. 2Lt E.M. Agnew joined and posted to A Coy.	[signature] Capt. A&SH

Instructions regarding War Diaries and Intelligence Summaries are contained in F. S. Regs., Part II. and the Staff Manual respectively. Title pages will be prepared in manuscript.

2 Original

WAR DIARY
or
~~INTELLIGENCE SUMMARY.~~
(*Erase heading not required.*)

Army Form C. 2118.

Hour, Date, Place		Summary of Events and Information	Remarks and references to Appendices
Oct 5th	Billets CHUIGNOLLES	Adjt. visited Gloster Regt's Hqrs in trenches to make arrangements for officers etc. to visit the front line trenches before battalion moved up. Captain R. S. Lindsay 9th The Royal Scots attached to Battalion for instruction in duties of adjutant. Working parties in the evening.	
Oct 6th	billets	C.O. adjt and usual representatives visited trenches in the morning. Trenches very intricate and difficult to learn. Working parties in the evening. 2Lt. J.M. Taylor bruised by fall of earth after a mine explosion. Baths for A Coy at PROYART.	
Oct 7th	billets	Baths for remainder of the battalion during the day. 2/Lt. W.S. Young joined and posted to C Coy. A draft of 29 arrived in the evening mostly men who had been at base recovering after wounds or sickness.	
Oct 8th	billets to trenches	Relieved Gloster Regt in trenches F1, F2, G1, G2 which were taken over by A, B, C, D Coys respectively. Hqrs. in large house FONTAINE les CAPPY. Relief was quick. A and B Coys warned to expect a mine explosion at junction of F1 and F2 trenches as enemy were thought to have completed their mine. The dangerous part of the line was therefore not	A R Boyle Capt 1/A&SH

(73989) W4141—463. 400,000. 9/14. H.&J.Ltd. Forms/C. 2118/10.

Instructions regarding War Diaries and Intelligence Summaries are contained in F. S. Regs., Part II. and the Staff Manual respectively. Title pages will be prepared in manuscript.

original
3

WAR DIARY
or
INTELLIGENCE SUMMARY.
(*Erase heading not required.*)

Army Form C. 2118.

Hour, Date, Place	Summary of Events and Information	Remarks and references to Appendices
Oct 8th continued	held but only patrolled at intervals - and dispositions made to counterattack at once should mine explode and enemy advance. A complicated line of trenches which will take long to learn. Mining activity has been great and in two places we hold one side of the mine crater and the enemy the other. 1 Coy 8th R.S.F. (Capt Rea commanding) attached, (two platoons to each of C and D Coys.) for instruction.	
Oct 9th Trenches	Normal routine trench work during the day. In the evening a sentry report that enemy had been seen cutting his wire prepared all for the explosion of the mine. Neighbouring units were warned and artillery asked to stand by. The report was false, but enemy were undoubtedly working at repair of their wire. A verbal report is fatal. Some bombing near the mine crater in G1 trench about 7 p.m. with no noticeable results.	Strength 25 officers 938 O.R.
Oct 10th Trenches.	Routine. The attached coy. 8th R.S.F. returned to billets. Guns registered during the afternoon - and in evening there was a lively bomb fight in front of F1 salient in which "A" Coy bombers showed much promise and energy.	
Oct 11th trenches.	A normal day. G.O.C. 81st I Bde visited trenches during the morning to see new retrenchment behind F1 salient - a most unsafe trench at present.	A R Boyle Capt 1/R.S.H.

Instructions regarding War Diaries and Intelligence Summaries are contained in F. S. Regs., Part II. and the Staff Manual respectively. Title pages will be prepared in manuscript.

Original 4

WAR DIARY
or
~~INTELLIGENCE SUMMARY.~~
(Erase heading not required.)

Army Form C. 2118.

Hour, Date, Place	Summary of Events and Information	Remarks and references to Appendices
Oct 12th trenches to CHUIGNOLLES	Daylight relief by Gloster Regt in the morning; very quick. marched back to former billets.	
Oct 13th billets	A normal day with working parties in the evening.	
Oct 14th billets	G.O.C. 27th Div (Maj. Gen. G. Milne D.S.O. C.B.) addressed all officers at Hqrs house at 5 p.m. He stated that a winter campaign was certain and that every effort was to be made to train young officers in leading men, initiative and power of command. The G.O.C 3rd Army had asked him to speak personally to all officers on these subjects and also on subject of drink amongst men, dress and general turn out. Working parties as usual.	
Oct 15th billets	G.O.C. 81st I.B. inspected Grenadier company at 2.30 p.m. in throwing dummy bombs, bombing a trench and other minor tactical schemes. The grenadier coy. as at present formed consists of 1 officer (Lt C.B Robertson) 1 sergt. (Anderson) 1 a/C.Q.M.S. (Sgt McLachlan) 1 N.C.O and 15 men from each company and a reserve of 4 men from each coy. A total of 1 officer and 82 O.R. The coy. is self contained except for pay - and seems to be a great success. In addition every subaltern, N.C.O and man in the battalion has a working knowledge of the Mills grenade.	A R Boyle Capt 1/A&SH.

(73989) W4141—463. 400,000. 9/14. H.&J.Ltd. Forms/C. 2118/10.

original

5.

WAR DIARY
or
~~INTELLIGENCE SUMMARY.~~

(*Erase heading not required.*)

Army Form C. 2118.

Instructions regarding War Diaries and Intelligence Summaries are contained in F. S. Regs., Part II. and the Staff Manual respectively. Title pages will be prepared in manuscript.

Hour, Date, Place	Summary of Events and Information	Remarks and references to Appendices
Oct 16th CHUIGNOLLES to trenches	Relieved Glosters in same trenches in the morning. D Coy to F1, A to F2, B to G1, C to G2. Suspected mine now reported to be non existent.	Strength 26 officers 921 O.R
Oct 17th trenches	A normal trench day. Platoon kitchens in trenches have replaced cookers which were ~~at~~ & near Hqrs in FONTAINE les CAPPY during the first tour 8th–12th	
Oct 18th trenches	A normal day. G.O.C 81st I.B visited Hqrs in the morning. Lt. Ritchie went on leave which reopened on 16th. Some bombing in the evening but without result	
Oct 19th trenches	G.O.C visited Hqrs in the morning. Lt. G. I. Campbell, Sgt Melville and Cpl left trenches and slept night at Hqrs leaving early on	
Oct 20th trenches	morning of 20th for ROUEN as instructors to details for 3 months. Relief by Gloster Regt completed by 11.30 a.m and battalion marched back to old billets in CHUIGNOLLES	
Oct 21st Billets	Routine work and cleaning up after trenches. News of approaching move received.	A.R. Boyle Capt 1/A&SH
Oct 22nd Billets	Various fatigue parties required during the day, which was otherwise spent getting ready to move.	

(73989) W4141—463. 400,000. 9/14. H.&J.Ltd. Forms/C. 2118/10.

Instructions regarding War Diaries and Intelligence Summaries are contained in F. S. Regs., Part II. and the Staff Manual respectively. Title pages will be prepared in manuscript.

6 Original

WAR DIARY
or
~~INTELLIGENCE SUMMARY.~~
(*Erase heading not required.*)

Army Form C. 2118.

Hour, Date, Place	Summary of Events and Information	Remarks and references to Appendices
Oct 23rd CHUIGNOLLES to MÉRICOURT	Left CHUIGNOLLES at 9 a.m and marched to MÉRICOURT the Hqrs of 27th Divn. Billets uncomfortable. Officers - Lt. Col. H. L. Henderson, Majors Elphinstone and Forbes. Capts Wilson Boyle (adjt) Greenfield MacKay, Lts Ritchie (on leave) Cunning Law (M.G.) Robertson (grenadier coy) Thorneycroft, 2Lts Agnew, McCutcheon, Berry, Gillespie, Neilson McAlister, Clark, Maclean, Younie, Surtees, Taylor, Gunn, [illegible] (Lt Rome sent home) 2Lts [illegible], Surtees, ~~[illegible]~~ McAlister all ~~[illegible]~~ under medical treatment and likely to be sent home.	Strength 23 Officers 970 O.R.
Oct 24th MÉRICOURT to LAMOTTE en SANTERRE	Left billets at 12 noon and marched to LAMOTTE occupying former billets. Rain came on about 1 p.m but not sufficiently to spoil the march	
Oct 25th billets	Nothing to report. Camerons and 9th R. Scots billetted in the village - and brigade Hqrs marched in during the morning	

A R Boyle Capt
1/A&SH.

(73989) W4141—463. 400,000. 9/14. H.&J.Ltd. Forms/C. 2118/10.

Army Form C. 2118.

Instructions regarding War Diaries and Intelligence Summaries are contained in F. S. Regs., Part II. and the Staff Manual respectively. Title pages will be prepared in manuscript.

7. Original

WAR DIARY or ~~INTELLIGENCE~~ SUMMARY.

(*Erase heading not required.*)

Hour, Date, Place	Summary of Events and Information	Remarks and references to Appendices
Oct 26th LAMOTTE en SANTERRE to BOVES Amiens map sheet 12; Montdidier sheet 21	Paraded 7.35 a.m and marched to BOVES where battalion was accommodated in tents pitched on a hill above the village. Companies marched at 200 yards interval 10 yards between platoons - five minutes between battalions. Passed G.O.C 27th Division at cross roads ½ mile N. of N in St. NICHOLAS east of BOVES (Montdidier sheet 21). Men marched well only 3 falling out. The grenadier coy as formerly constituted ceased to exist to-day and grenadier formation was composed as follows - 1 officer 2 sergeants and 8 O.R attached to H.qrs and each platoon ~~with~~ 1 N.C.O and 8 men as company grenadiers. Authority. A.O.1 d 1/x/15/	
Oct 27th BOVES to BOUGAINVILLE	Paraded 7.30 a.m and marched to BOUGAINVILLE 11 miles West of AMIENS (Amiens sheet 12). Route BOVES - ST. FUSCIEN - DURY - VERS - CLAIRY - PISSY FLUY - BOUGAINVILLE. Halted 1½ hours at PISSY for dinners. Reached billets about 3.30 pm. Fairly comfortable. March 17 miles. 10 men fell out and were carried part of the way in an ambulance but all marched last 5 miles. Many of those who fell out were men classified as unfit for duty and normally employed in Divisional baths, sanitary squads etc.	A R Boyle Capt 1/A&SH

Instructions regarding War Diaries and Intelligence Summaries are contained in F. S. Regs., Part II. and the Staff Manual respectively. Title pages will be prepared in manuscript.

original
8.

WAR DIARY
or
~~INTELLIGENCE SUMMARY.~~
(Erase heading not required.)

Army Form C. 2118.

Hour, Date, Place	Summary of Events and Information	Remarks and references to Appendices
Oct 28th billets	Day spent settling down and re arranging billets after Camerons had marched to other billets in ST AUBAIN. Two piquets posted on roads N. of village to prevent men straying out of Divisional area. The battalion has not been so far from the trenches since Dec 21st 1914.	
Oct 29th billets	Routine work only. Nothing to report.	
Oct 30th billets	Companies worked independantly – Bomb, signallers and machine gun classes busy. All men considered unfit seen by A.D.M.S and many marked P.B. which means they are sent to the base.	Strength 23 officers 967 O.R.
Oct 31st billets	A cold wet day. Church parade at 11.45 a.m. in the open. Nothing else to report. A canteen and recreation room found for the men and fitted with tables etc	

A R Boyle Capt
1/R.S.F. [illegible]

www.ingramcontent.com/pod-product-compliance
Lightning Source LLC
Chambersburg PA
CBHW081544160426
43191CB00011B/1837